The
Great
Prize
Fight

By Alan Lloyd, also published by Souvenir Press Ltd

MARATHON
DESTROY CARTHAGE
THE TARAS REPORT ON THE LAST DAYS OF POMPEII

The Great Prize Fight

Alan Lloyd

SOUVENIR PRESS

Copyright © 1977 Alan Lloyd

First published in Great Britain in 1977 by Cassell & Co.

This paperback edition published 2004 by
Souvenir Press Ltd
42 Great Russell Street
London WC1 3PR

The right of Alan Lloyd to be identified as the author of this work has
been asserted by him in accordance with the Copyright, Designs and
Patents Act, 1988.

ISBN 0 285 63705 3

Printed and bound in Great Britain by
Cox & Wyman Ltd, Reading, Berkshire

For my father

RICHARD LLOYD

Contents

PART III AND THE JAWS CRACKLE

APPENDIXES

In a word—I trust I shall always
be found at the Scratch with Honour
PIERCE EGAN

Author's note

Since my searches for the long forgotten and largely untold story of the great title fight of 1860—in effect, the first world championship contest—began at the grave of Tom Sayers, it is fitting that my obligation should be expressed initially to the Highgate Cemetery Company, London, and Mr Curvey, whose prompt inquiries yielded important clues. No ally could have taken up the trail more diligently than New Scotland Yard, and my thanks are due to the Metropolitan Police Office for generous and thorough archive investigations on my behalf. In the sporting world, I am particularly indebted to the British Boxing Board of Control, and its General Secretary, Mr R. L. Clarke, for the time and facilities they gave me. I am also appreciative of the advice given by Group Captain H. A. F. Summers, C.B.E., of the National Sporting Club, and my friend and respected sports journalist John Ballantine. To Celia the Dowager Lady Noble, J.P., whose informative sources are as unfailing as her charm, I am indebted for the loan of volumes from her collection of Victorian writing. Swift and efficient help in tracing American records was provided by the United States Embassy, London, and the Reference and Research Library of the United States Information Service, London, and I am grateful to the staffs involved. Hampshire yielded assistance in several quarters. To the Hampshire County Council I owe thanks for both advice and information, particular indebtedness being due to Philip Costello, press officer, Miss M. E. Cash, county archivist, and her assistant, Miss S. J. Berry. At the *Hampshire Chronicle*, Gracia Woodhouse, the editor, and her staff, gave up time to search their files and make notes for me, a courtesy greatly appreciated, as was the trouble taken by the editor of the *Farnborough Mail* to seek out and express me information. For invaluable pointers and his friendly interest, I am indebted to Edward Hutt, honorary secretary of the Farnborough Historical Society, only regretting that lack of time curtailed further exchanges. On the subject of fight excursions and railway companies, I received generous assistance from the British Railways Board, through Mr D. L. Joiner, and from a number of specialist historians and enthusiasts. My gratitude is due especially to Alan Voce, honorary secretary of the Railway and Canal Historical Society, to Professor H. P. White of the University of Salford, and to Mr H. V. Borley, for sparing time to offer me expert advice on railway matters. As usual, I received nothing but help and expeditious service from the staffs of the London Library, the British Library and the Public Records Office; also the British Transport Historical Records Office and the National Newspaper Library at Colindale. To these, and the innumerable book specialists and antiquaries who responded manfully to my inquiries, I extend my thanks. Finally, to Daphne, for so much that made another book possible, my love and appreciation.

ALAN LLOYD
Kent, 1976

Prologue

Adah Isaacs Menken, the original 'Naked Lady' of the show world, died in August 1868 aged thirty-three. The weather in Paris that month was as torrid as summer in her own Louisiana. From her bedroom three stories above the rue Caumartin, the tumult of human affairs below seemed distant. For days, lying in pain and solitude, the rewards of fame squandered, Menken had awaited the last calls of admirers—the valedictions of the four men she had married, and many others she had intimately favoured. None climbed the stairs from the street to her bedside. Neither James Barkley, a rich Californian and her latest husband, nor Alexandre Dumas senior, whose mistress she had been recently, attended her. Nor did Charles Reade or Algernon Swinburne, the literary celebrities whose protestations of affection were still fresh. Nor Charles Dickens, who had enjoyed her company in London and was in Paris as she lay sick. It was 4 p.m. on the 10th when Menken, alone save for a distraught maid, succumbed to the cancer in her left breast.

Charles Reade noted her passing in his diary thus: 'A clever woman with beautiful eyes—very dark blue. A bad actress . . . talked well and was intelligent in private. She spoilt her looks off stage with white lead, or whatever else it is these idiots of women wear. She did not rouge, but played some devilry with her glorious eyes, which altogether made her spectral. She wrote poetry. It was as bad as other people's—would have been worse if it could—*Requiescat in Pace*. Goodish heart. Loose conduct. Gone!'

That Menken's fame—her notoriety, as many would have had it—derived from her body and not her mind was a constant regret to her. Tossing her dark hair, puffing the cigar she affected, she would sip the brandy of some grateful management and bemoan the neglect of her creative soul. She had left New Orleans as a girl to offer her genius to humankind, but the gift had been overlooked. 'You know,' she wrote by way of explanation, 'how difficult it is for an actress to get an opening in any theatre where she has no position, no matter what talents she may possess.' Reade's assessment of her talents was accurate. Where her charm wheedled roles, the results were deplorable. At Nashville, her Lady Macbeth was a travesty—'full of southern passion', allowed one writer, 'but devoid of Shakespeare or, for that matter, any known playwright'. In New York, her Lady Teazle was disastrous.

It was left to James Murdoch, an experienced actor who had suffered the misfortune to appear with her, to tell Menken the blunt truth. She should, he said bravely, for her temper was volatile, forget acting and exploit her small, voluptuous figure in 'spectaculars'.

About the same time—it was 1861, and the shadow of civil war threatened America—an enterprising impresario, Captain John B. Smith of Albany, was staging a popular diversion called *Mazeppa*, an old-time thriller loosely based on Byron's romance of Ivan Mazeppa, a Tartar prince taken captive by his enemies. The show depended for its main appeal on a sequence in which the prince, stripped and lashed to an untamed steed by his captors, supposedly was borne headlong into the distant hills. To satisfy his audiences, Smith had trained a placid mare named Beauty to trot up a wooden ramp between painted mountains with a bare-limbed actor across her back, secured by a special girth. The inspiration that this sensation might be enhanced by replacing the actor with a woman was clinched for Smith when he met Menken. Apprehensively, she accepted and rehearsed the unlikely role.

The first public performance of *Mazeppa* with Menken taking the lead in silk fleshings was given at Smith's Green Street Theatre, Albany, that June. In an age when the female form was habitually encased in clothing from neck to toe—when the display of an ankle was daring, and many husbands had never seen their wives undressed—the appearance of Menken in tights, on her back across a horse, was breathtaking. Even in a city of staid tradition, the home of puritanical Dutch stock, the show was an instant hit. 'The Naked Lady' became an institution overnight. Awake to her potential, Smith lengthened the ramp and made it zigzag, at once increasing the eroticism and duration of Menken's ride.

It proved longer than even Captain Smith imagined. Pittsburg, St

Louis, Cincinnati were conquered. Publicity multiplied. Much of it could be summarized in the words of a Californian editor: 'Menken's exhibitions are unfit for the public eye; degrading to the drama whose temples they defile; a libel upon women whose sex is hereby depraved and whose chastity is corrupted'. Smith rubbed his hands. As Beauty clopped patiently from state to state, the box-office takings soared. New York's Broadway Theatre was the first to pay Menken the then staggering sum of 500 dollars a performance. Greater riches lay overseas. London, Paris, Vienna flocked to *Mazeppa*. Charles Dickens was among those turned away from Royal Astley's in Westminster Bridge Road when Menken—now billed as 'The Most Successful Star of the Age'—opened there to a full house.

She made the most of her celebrity, living and spending flamboyantly. Between performances in London, she rode splendidly accoutred in Rotten Row, surrounded by a posse of courtiers. In Paris she drove her own gilded chariot nightly to the Gaîeté, cracking her whip above a team of thoroughbreds. The boldest daughters of the *demi-monde* were eclipsed. Cora Pearl and Alice Ozy might have been more beautiful, La Barucci and La Paiva more mysterious, but Menken gave the public incomparable value, not only on stage but in her private life. Husbands and lovers succeeded one another with scandalous celerity. Though few of her escorts were rich men, they abounded in genius, the dramatic and literary talents Menken had always prized. In their company, she sought to assert her intellectual self; to patch over the vulgar flaw in her own success. When she failed, she fell into black moods.

These deepened as her health began to deteriorate. Too often her talented companions enjoyed her favours and laughed at her pretensions, not least her attempt to play the role of a later-day Madame de Staël. Swinburne, who pursued her with undignified ardour, tried to pass it off later as his pity for a poor tart. Menken clung to her delusions to the bitter end. 'I am lost to art and life,' she declared when the medical prognosis was known to her. Already, a score of imitators was ready to take her place—Mazeppas of many shapes. The world released her, as it had greeted her early efforts, with indifference. Fifteen people, including the hearse grooms, bearers and her maid, were at the funeral.

'Not a single actress present!' exclaimed a lone voice in *Figaro*.

3

'Where were you, all you good friends of Menken—and you directors, authors and journalists who have so often sung the beauty of the American equestrienne?'

Amid the silence which ensued, an incident occurred in England, heeded only by its participants, which threw a curious sidelight on Menken's life. Returning to London by train from Doncaster races, a retired bruiser named Jem Mace saw a notice of her death in a paper. Two drunks in the carriage were discussing the day's sport in foul language. Appealing to their better feelings, Mace explained that he was mourning the loss of a friend, and would be glad if they would stop cursing. Since they took no regard, and the train had halted for water, Mace dragged the larger of the two outside, thumped him severely, and resumed his journey undisturbed.

Jem Mace, semi-illiterate and ham-fisted, was one of a number of pugs Menken's friends might have recalled frequenting the theatres at which she played. Her familiarity with them had irked her regular coterie. Servants would stiffen and raise disapproving eyebrows at the thickset, coarse-mannered men, lumpy in their flash suits, who periodically had turned up in her company. Menken had seldom talked of them. For a night or two, they would empty the decanters in her elegant dressing-rooms, or sprawl on her soft divan. Then they would go again. Once only, in her recorded observations, is there reference to this phenomenon. In an unguarded moment she confided that the sole experience of real love in her life was for a pugilist. Among the few personal possessions she left in Paris were a number of golden trinkets, a Hebrew bible and a fading copy of the *New York Herald* of 29 April 1860. It was a special Sunday edition devoted to the greatest prize-fight of the century.

I THE BRUISERS

Hurrah for the Ring and the bunch of fives!

PUGILISTICA

1 Burke and Bendigo

> *In evil long I took delight,*
> *I used to glory in a fight;*
> *But Jesus stopped me on the way*
> *And bid me work and watch and pray.*
> CHORUS: *So I'll win the day . . .*
> > 'The Bendigo Song'

Among the earliest events in Adah Menken's memory was the visit to New Orleans in 1837 of a British fist-fighter named James Burke. Though Englishmen had been prize-fighting since the seventeenth century, the sport was then young in America—a native champion had yet to be recognized—and a professional pugilist was a newsworthy oddity in the south. Oddity was part of Burke's stock-in-trade. Congenital deafness, remarked in his billing as 'The Deaf 'un' or 'Deaf Burke', had produced an abnormality of speech and manner which, perhaps from simplicity of mind or defensiveness, he cultivated as burlesque. Before an audience, Burke would cavort like a large child.. He had been known to appear at the ringside with his face daubed in the fashion of a circus clown. By contrast, the twelve stone of muscle and sinew he carried composed a force which had consigned his last opponent to violent death.

Subsequent difficulties in obtaining a match nearer home had brought Burke to the United States, where the absence of professionals on the East Coast induced him to travel south. The citizens of New Orleans were to forget neither Burke nor their first taste of prize-fighting for a long time. Having received a challenge from an itinerant brawler named Sam O'Rourke, then living locally, the Englishman agreed to a contest on 5 May. The advantage in skill was with Burke; O'Rourke had the backing. The Mississippi wharves and

7

shanties were thick with Irish immigrants, of proverbial clannishness and hot blood. On 13 May, the *Charleston Courier* ran the following report from New Orleans, dated 6 May:

For some two or three days past, large numbers of our population have been thrown into considerable excitement by handbills posted in bar-rooms and at the corners of streets [intimating] that a pugilistic combat was to take place yesterday between two prize-fighters, Deaf Burke, an Englishman, and O'Rourke, an Irishman. The fight took place at about one o'clock, at the forks of the Bayou Road. Some two or three rounds were fought, to the particular advantage of neither of the belligerents. The second of O'Rourke, happening to come within hitting distance of Burke, received a severe blow from the deaf man. This was the signal for a general scrimmage in which the Irishmen joined O'Rourke, attacking Burke and his friends with fists and sticks . . . .

According to another version, O'Rourke's second, Mick Carson, had pushed Burke from behind, propelling him into his opponent's arms. On Burke informing Carson he would knock him down if he repeated the incident, Carson allegedly replied that if Burke touched him he would slit the Englishman's gizzard—an ominous possibility since Carson, like many in the predominantly Irish and creole crowd, carried a knife. Indeed, he possessed not only a knife but a pistol. Having flattened him before he could put either to misuse, Burke prudently fled from the hostile mob.

Matters [*continued the* Courier] were coming to a fine pass. Burke was followed by a crowd of Irishmen with shillelaghs, dray-pins, whips and other weapons. A well-wisher, seeing him pass, handed him a bowie knife, and another gave him a horse, on which he escaped to New Orleans. The man who handed Burke the knife was cruelly beaten by friends of O'Rourke, and we fear killed. On the arrival of the different parties in town, inflamed by liquor, many affrays occurred. During the whole afternoon, large numbers of malcontents, principally Irishmen, were congregated in the vicinity of the Union House, and Armstrong's, opposite the American

Theatre. Several serious and disgraceful fights took place, in some of which the mob beat and otherwise maltreated unoffending individuals. A large number of arrests were made. At eight o'clock in the evening, the Washington Guards were ordered out. . . .

Retreating hastily to New York, Burke agreed to fight another Irishman, O'Connell, to prove his value in fair contest. Notwithstanding a sheriff's notice in anticipation of more riots, the fight took place without interruption on Hart's Island, where Burke made short work of an unprofessional adversary. It was, as one commentator expressed it, 'a doubloon to a shin-plaster, and no takers'. But it did provide the American Press with something better than the debacle at New Orleans on which to pass judgement. The *New York Herald* was equivocal:

Although we regret and detest such exhibitions, our duty as chroniclers compels us to make public what otherwise we should bury in oblivion. . . . The ancient Romans conquered and civilized half the world, and it is to them we owe the gladiatorial spectacle of the Prize Ring—modified by modern civilization yet retaining sufficient of its origin to portray the manners and habits of the people among whom it has taken root. The British people are particularly fond of this exhibition, and there are some good consequences attending it. Three or four [people] do not fall upon and beat a single individual. The single man when struck down by his opponent is permitted to rise and put himself, as it were, in something like a state of equilibrium . . . and when the party combating cries, 'Hold, enough!' no bowie knife enters his vitals. With all its disadvantages, therefore, and demoralizing tendency, it may be doubted whether the spirit emanating from it may not be productive of benefit among the lower classes.

In fact, fist-fighting was much older than the Roman empire, being amply witnessed in Homer and Virgil. Its appeal to the British was true enough. From the fall of Rome to the beginning of the nineteenth century, pugilism seems to have been unknown among civilized nations with the single exception of England. Burke, outclassing the opposition he encountered in America, was himself outclassed in

Britain on his return in 1838. In his own words, he had hurried home to 'take the shine out of little fry who used my absence to bounce and crow like cocks in a gutter'. But Burke belonged to the thirties; the men of the forties had come of age. In February 1839, the new decade was signalled near Appleby, Warwickshire, where Burke's career was effectively terminated in ten rounds by a Nottingham roughneck known as Bendigo.

*

At this point in its history, the focus of prize-fighting diffused swiftly from its old Thames-side citadels—the London slums and sporting dens that had spawned Burke and a legion of bygone pugs—to encompass new frontiers. In the United States, isolated bands of fight-followers discovered common interest in the mounting reputations of such American fighters as Tom Hyer and James Ambrose (Yankee Sullivan), who had some claim to be the first native champions. In 1842, an American ventured his luck in the English ring, proving more a sensation than a national threat. Charles Freeman, the 'New World Atlas', was seven feet tall and weighed twenty-three stone on arrival, though he reduced to about eighteen stone in training. Immensely strong, he was also pacific by temperament, a showman rather than a pugilist.

In exhibition bouts at the Queen's Theatre, Liverpool, and several London houses, Freeman was a great success, but two contests in earnest with an English opponent, William Perry, the 'Tipton Slasher', ended in fiasco. Conceding five stone and a foot in height, Perry could make little impression on Freeman. Freeman lacked the aggression to stop the Slasher. The first match dragged on until enveloping fog obscured the ring, and the fight was abandoned. The second was awarded to Freeman on a technical foul by his adversary, a result the giant received with suitable modesty, expressing his gratitude to all involved. It was his last fight. He died three years later at Winchester, Hampshire, of consumption, his end accelerated by exposure to the draughts of successive theatres and circuses, in which he had appeared clad merely in spangled tights.

In England, the drift of prize-fighting through the forties, reflecting a slump in London patronage, favoured its Midland fans. Nottingham was noted for its fighters. Industrialized, radical, not infrequently riotous, the city possessed a belligerent populace all too fond of violence. Both Benjamin Caunt and Bendigo Thompson, the outstanding bruisers of the decade, were men of Nottingham. Caunt, big, hard and unsentimental, visited America in 1841 without receiving a serious challenge. For a time he appeared at the Bowery Theatre in a show called *Life in London*, displaying his muscle in a scene depicting the sparring-room of Tom Cribb, a veteran champion then still living in Panton Street, off Haymarket. But it was Caunt's smaller fellow-townsman and rival, the vanquisher of Deaf Burke, who dominated the years to 1850.

Bendigo's renown, spreading far beyond the sporting fraternity of his day, owed much to a dramatic espousal of respectability in middle-age. Appealing to the reforming zeal of the period, it produced not one but two legends, elevating his fame from back-street and tap-room to the parlours of bourgeois society. Arthur Conan Doyle, who commended the champion's memory to middle-class manhood, opened a poem called *Bendy's Sermon* with the lines: 'You didn't know of Bendigo! Well, that knocks me out! / Who's your board school teacher? What's he been about?' Few outside the sub-culture of the fighting world had seemed likely to interest themselves in the close-coupled Nottingham tearaway during his early life.

William Thompson, born in 1811, the youngest of triplets—hence the sobriquet Abednego or Bendigo—came of a family of twenty-one children and a strikingly split disposition. Part of the clan, taking after the father, a hard-working artisan, was earnest, knowledge-seeking and equable. One or more sons preached in the Non-Conformist chapels of the neighbourhood. The other part, encouraged by Mrs Thompson, whose post-procreative years appear to have been spent scanning boxing journals and smoking a clay pipe, was violent. Bendigo, too late in the nursery to receive an education, grew up illiterate. Consigned briefly to the workhouse on the death of his father, the boy emerged from its rigours determined his mother should never end up there. At sixteen, he entered, and won, his first fight for money. 'I did it to get a living,' he said later. 'It came natural. I did it for my mother.'

Five feet nine in height, between eleven and twelve stone, Bendigo almost always fought heavier opponents, and almost always bested them. A contemporary artist depicted him with dark hair in a short fringe, angular, somewhat clerical features, square shoulders and powerful arms. He fought southpaw, fists chest-high, and he hit very dangerously with both hands. Perhaps his biggest asset was his natural quick-wittedness, a quality rare among pugilists. Few were men of much cerebral subtlety. To their confusion, and the fury of their ringside friends, Bendigo waged psychological as well as physical warfare in the prize-ring, taunting his opponents with insults and grimaces. Agility enabled him to dodge the enraged response before coolly flighting his own punch. He was, said one, 'as deadly as a tarantula spider'.

The epic battles of his career were with his Nottingham rival, Caunt, then based in London as landlord of the Coach and Horses, St Martin's Lane. Caunt, whose father had worked for Lord Byron, a keen amateur pugilist, towered over Bendigo, two stone heavier, six inches to spare in height. The deciding struggle—fought to the verge of exhaustion on both sides at Sutfield Green, near Oxford, in 1845—assured Bendigo the championship. In the course of the contest he was hit with a bludgeon by one of Caunt's supporters. He left the battlefield closely protected by friendly roughs. So fearful on occasions were his brothers for his safety that they supposedly connived at his arrest to stop him fighting.

His mother, on the other hand, egged him on. In later days, Bendigo liked to recall how Mrs Thompson, as a crone in her eighties, coerced him into his final match. He was forty at the time, semi-crippled with a gammy leg. 'I found her at her lodgings smoking her pipe and reading a sporting sheet. "Have you seen this?" she says. (It referred to a challenge from a younger boxer.) "No," I says. "Hmm," says she. "A fellow with no more breadth to his shoulders than there is between the eyes of a mouse, and he dares to challenge you. . . . Well, I tell you, if you won't fight him, I'll challenge him to fight myself."' Bendigo duly fought. Giving weight, fifteen years and half a leg, he took the verdict.

In 1850, having beaten every major heavyweight in England, Bendigo Thompson retired from the prize-ring. He did not stop brawling. Purchasing an expensive paunch at the Three Crowns, Parliament Street, and other Nottingham ale-bars, he was quick to involve himself in street fights, and to lend his muscle at election times. In his own words: 'I took to drinking heavy, and gambling and jollying. I was in and out of the House of Correction.' But for the intervention of a noted Nottingham reformer and revivalist, Richard Weaver, Bendigo must have ended, like many a former fighter, as a common criminal or mendicant.

Weaver had other plans. Revivalist preachers, then commanding large followings in many communities, vied to produce colourful converts on their platforms. Weaver, an ex-collier familiar with hard cases, knew a prospect when he saw one. Incorrigible as the bruiser at first seemed, the stamp of his kin and intelligence marked him as retrievable. Helped by an earlier convert, an acquaintance of Bendigo's named John Dupee, the missionary set out to tame the erstwhile champion. It was a long tussle. Stories survive of how Weaver was knocked flat by Bendigo; how the novitiate was first fascinated by a sermon on David and Goliath, whom he likened to himself and his rival, Caunt; how, as his faith grew, Bendigo would strip off his jacket in the presence of atheists and raise his fists.

Doubtless, some of the tales were apocryphal, but it is certain that the process of conversion, long and arduous, justified Weaver's local nickname of 'Dauntless Dick'. After several relapses and subsequent rescues by his new friends, Bendigo appeared and spoke with increasing zeal on religious platforms. Wrote a journalist who met him after his regeneration: 'I found a comfortable-looking gentleman with his legs crossed in an easy-chair in a manner which unmistakably betokened how kindly he had taken to his new career. He was full of modesty and good nature, and had the cheery aspect of an English country squire.' He was not, however, complacent. London, and its daunting sins, were to be his next challenge. He was ready for the affray. 'My Christian friends, I was never a coward in the Devil's cause; I do not mean to be a coward in Christ's cause.'

Bendigo's proselytization from arch-exponent of violence to the ranks of moral rectitude personified a growing conflict in British public attitudes. 'Life,' declared the English statesman and author Sir George Cornewall Lewis, 'would be tolerable were it not for its pleasures.'

As a reaction to the vulgar and often cruel diversions of a changing age, it was a sentiment held by more and more Victorians. By Bendigo's retirement, mid-century, prize-fighting was under hostile pressure from what one sports editor impugned as 'this Puritanical campaign against the amusements and relaxations of the people'. Increasingly, magistracy and police invoked the law of breach of peace against the prize-ring. Pugilism had become a battle on two fronts.

2 The Belt

Let lobsters sore, with their truncheons, roar
'Disperse' to the pugilistic corps—
The pinks of the Prize Ring, in freedom nurs'd
Shall tell them undaunted to do their worst.
          Chant of the Victorian ring

On the afternoon of 16 December 1851—a raw day, steamy with the breath of men and horses—Tom Paddock, a professional fighter and farm worker from Redditch, fought a Nottingham railway navvy, Harry Poulson, at Cross End, near Belper, Derbyshire. The scene was fairly typical of the fifties prize-ring. The venue was a meadow devoted to winter keep. Ropes strung on eight stakes formed the regulation quadrangle, twenty-four by twenty-four feet. In the centre a line, the scratch, had been scuffed in the damp turf. Other lines, at the corners, marked spaces for the seconds, who would stay in the ring while the rounds were fought. To his own corner-post, each fighter had attached a handkerchief in his battle colours.

Bare-fisted, stripped from the waist up, the combatants wore close-fitting drawers, high stockings and spiked boots. Paddock was the taller, a beefy man with a heavy, bucolic face. Poulson, six years the senior at thirty-three, was stocky with apprehensive features and a deep chest. Both weighed a pound or so more than twelve stone. The fight began at one o'clock, Paddock gaining the first knock-down with a shot in Poulson's left eye. At this, the stricken man's second and bottle-holder hauled him to his corner where, perched on the knee of a kneeling attendant, he received sponge and towel therapy. Rounds in the prize-ring were not of set duration but continued until a fighter was on the ground. His corner then had half a minute to revive him and return him to scratch, or concede defeat.

The fight lasted ninety-five minutes. Long before that, the damage was grisly. With no system of scoring, no limit to the rounds involved, the contest became a battle of attrition with exhaustion playing an increasing role. Neither man boxed for a knock-out. Both knew that, while the half-minute count curtailed the chances of a *coup de grâce*, big punching invited knuckle injury, a disastrous circumstance in the ring. Instead, the pugilists went for soft targets, chiselling at nerves, heart and kidneys, 'rabbit' punching, holding-and-hitting. They also hugged and threw the opponent, 'accidentally' falling on him. Surreptitious use was made of spiked boots.

Their seconds, tight-lipped men in fur caps and shirtsleeves, encouraged them. Outside the ring, a clearing measuring ten feet from the ropes contained two well wrapped umpires, one approved by each corner, and a referee sporting a top hat. Bearers of water and stronger refreshment for the fighters used the clearing, but spectators were banned from it. To emphasize the ruling, the ring-keepers, a squad of professional bruisers armed with metal-bound sticks and whips, patrolled in front of the assembled crowd.

The mob was a motley one. Rowdy contingents from rival camps, including Nottingham's notorious 'lambs', the most barbaric fight fans in the Midlands, obtrusively declared themselves. Handkerchiefs were waved which matched those in the corners, hawked for shillings by the fighters before the match. In the forward stations—secured by cash but quickly threatened by the scrum behind—a smattering of toppers, frock-coats and greatcoats indicated the presence of gentlemen: florid landlords, hunting parsons, city punters out for coarse sport. Hired pugs acted as bodyguards for the older ones. Less conspicuously, pick-pockets thrived on the heave and crush—'flimps' who specialized in the subtleties of crowd work; common 'gonophs' who grabbed and ran. For all the prevalence of top-coats at the meeting, complaints of missing seals and gold hunters were numerous.

While the fight progressed, gambling preoccupied the affluent. Betting was brisk between spectators, often for large amounts. Not only the toffs, but dubious men with greasy side-whiskers—Newgate knockers—and flash hats, flourished wads of fivers and long-tails. To the fighters, the battle stakes of £100 seemed riches, but the loser reckoned on none of it, unless the winner cared to spare a pound or two.

Two familiar contingencies quickly imposed themselves. Barely had the first blood issued from Poulson's nose than the mob surged forward for a closer view. Ignoring the lashings of the ring-whips, backers and fans engulfed the corners of their favourites, some brandishing cudgels across the ropes. Prudently, the fighters held mainly to the middle ground, retreating when in trouble but seldom advancing much beyond the scratch mark. At the same time four Derbyshire magistrates and the Chief Constable of Belper, William Wragg, reached Cross End and rode to the battlefield. The fixture had been known to the Derbyshire, Nottinghamshire and Leicestershire authorities for several days, but the venue had eluded them until the last moment. Without delaying to assemble a police force, the magistrates had collected Wragg and spurred to Cross End.

Finding the fight in progress, one of their number, Jedediah Strutt, rode forward and commanded the crowd to disperse. The mob ignored him. Paddock seemed inclined to stop fighting at the order, but his backers urged him gruffly to carry on. As the contest continued, Strutt was seen to hesitate. The nearest substantial police reinforcement lay at Derby, eight miles distant. At length, he resolved to read the Riot Act. Accompanied by Wragg, who attempted to clear a path, Strutt nudged his horse through the crowd towards the prize-ring. Cries of 'Maw-worms!' (an abuse applied to hostile magistrates by fight enthusiasts) and 'Keep them out!' were followed by cudgel blows, and the constable disappeared amid a gang of some fifty roughs. Moments later, he sprawled senseless beneath his horse. At this, the magistrates withdrew with their casualty, one galloping directly to Derby.

Fearful of retribution, the crowd began to break up. Allowing Paddock the verdict, Poulson's corner, followed by umpires, backers and riff-raff, streamed away across the surrounding wurzel and turnip fields, down cart-tracks and country lanes. Many, in a variety of conveyances, made for Derby, the rail link to Nottingham. They found the borough constabulary waiting. Paddock was apprehended in a cab with his attendants; Poulson with friends in a spattered four-wheeler. According to report, the victor was contrite. 'He said he was sorry the p'liceman was hurt; and that he would have given over when the magistrate ordered, but was told by the gents he would lose the purse.'

The county court showed little sympathy. Weeks later, the pugilists were hauled from detention and, to the satisfaction of many pacific citizens, each sentenced to ten months' imprisonment with hard labour. Harsher than any penalty yet imposed on prize-fighters in breach of the public peace, the decision horrified the sporting world.

*

Few places reflected the declining reputation of pugilism more succinctly than Limmer's Hotel, the London rendezvous of well-to-do sportsmen on the corner of Hanover Square and Conduit Street. At Limmer's, a name as synonymous with sport in its day as Tattersall's and Weatherby's, the celebrated head waiter John Collins was said to have first compounded gin, soda-water, ice, lemon and sugar in a drink which had captured the taste of rich Americans. In the low-ceilinged coffee-room, such men as Lord Queensberry, Sir Edward Kent, the Marquis of Waterford, Lord George Bentinck and Lord Longford had publicly owned their part in the organization of prize-fights. That day had passed when Paddock and Poulson fought. By 1850, a peer of the realm would no more have presented his favourite bruiser at Limmer's than have allowed his name to appear in the boxing columns of *Sportsman's Magazine* or *Bell's Life*.

The group of prize-ring patrons who met at Limmer's soon after the release from prison of the Cross End offenders did so anonymously. Their concern was to discuss the disrepute of the fist-sport and seek a likely antidote. Older members could recall the Prince Regent and his brothers at the ringside. Eighteen of the nation's best pugilists, they remembered, had served as ushers at the Prince's coronation as George IV. The lustre of the past lingered in such names as Jack Broughton, the great coach and theorist; Tom Molyneaux, the masterly Negro; Death Oliver; Henry Pearce, the 'Game Chicken'; Dutch Sam; Peter Crawley, 'Young Rump Steak'; Spider Hoiles and the Gasman. Gentlemen had entered the ring themselves. Lord Byron and Sir Robert Peel had raised their fists as amateurs. Charles James Fox, William Wyndham, Lord Althorp and many others had enthusiastically followed the knuckle game.

But much had changed since Victoria's accession. Whereas elegant women of the twenties had driven to prize-fights escorted by 'the brilliant of the highest class', as the father of boxing writers, Pierce Egan, had put it, now the most degraded of females would run from a fight mob. Whereas newspapers had once extolled the 'manly virtues' of pugilism, now they tended to stress its mortal dangers, reminding their readers, for instance, that Bill Phelps of Brighton had been punched to death in '38 by Owen Swift; that Simon Byrne, killed in contest with Deaf Burke, had himself slaughtered M'Kay on the roped turf. While the greatest in the land had favoured fighters, the law had moved warily. By the fifties, to the frustration of the patrons at Limmer's, magisterial caution had disappeared. Police harassment was making prize-fighting a furtive sport.

The return of royal patronage was unthinkable. Nobody at Limmer's, or anywhere else, could imagine the earnest Prince Consort, let alone his wife, at the ringside. Bourgeois respectability, the new force, obliged public men of all ranks to indulge the pleasures enjoyed by their forebears with increasing stealth. Lords and statesmen still numbered in the Fancy, as the fight-audience termed itself, but their interest was unpublicized. Tactfully, sporting journals omitted the names of ringsiders from their reports. Aristocrats whose fathers would have disdained condemnation from any source rushed to print to deny their attendance at prize-fights.

What was needed, the friends of pugilism judged after due debate, was a symbol of prestige to uplift the sport. Proceeding from this conclusion, a subscription was opened in London in 1855 for a championship trophy of unprecedented distinction; an emblazoned belt of unsurpassed attraction in the fighting world.

Its manufacture was entrusted to Hancock's, the New Bond Street goldsmiths, and the news proclaimed in the sporting press of Britain and America. The new belt was put up for any pugilist, of any weight (fighters were not then classified in official weight groups) and any nationality, prepared to fight for it in open challenge on English soil. The holder should be bound to meet every challenge in the sum of not less than £200 a side, within six months of formal issue. Finally, 'any pugilist having held the belt against all comers for three years, without defeat, shall be its absolute possessor'.

The trophy won instant and widespread attention. Novice fighters beheld a new horizon in their affairs; old campaigners stirred to fresh endeavours. Among the veterans in England roused by the challenge were two former champions: Harry Broome of Birmingham, a lantern-jawed heavyweight, and the American Freeman's old opponent Perry, the Tipton Slasher, a lumbering son of the Black Country. Among the younger 'heavies', Aaron Jones, a skilful if somewhat unlucky tactician, glimpsed the chance of contention, as did Tom Paddock. Since emerging from prison, Paddock had embellished his Midlands reputation with a further win over Poulson. According to *Sportsman's Magazine*, the ruddy countryman learned of the belt with such excitement that 'his hair stood on end between hope and trepidation'.

For his own part, Poulson, jolted by two defeats and the rigours of imprisonment, returned to railway navvying. It was a hard school. So promiscuous was violence in the navvy camps that tough contractors and gang bosses were frightened to enter them. But if Poulson was unlikely to grow soft, the belt seemed remote to him. His sponsors proposed an easy match to boost his confidence. To this end, they came up with an indigent scrapper named Sayers, two stone lighter than Poulson and willing to meet him for low stakes. Tom Sayers, by trade a bricklayer from Camden Town, North London, was on hard times. At twenty-eight, he had beaten too many men at around his own weight of ten stone twelve to find takers under eleven stone. When he suggested fighting a bigger man, he got no backers. His friends protested loudly at the Poulson match, but Sayers contrived to scratch up the stake.

Though much of the Fancy, especially the heavyweight following, had seen little of Sayers, form suggested his telling punch. He was one of the few contemporary pugilists with a record of knock-out victories. In 1853, he had stopped one Jack Martin with a blow which had left him senseless for five minutes. In '54, George Sims, a long-reaching middleweight, had dropped to Sayers in the fourth round. From that point, the Camden Town fighter had searched the country without discovering an adversary in his own league. Beset by money and domestic troubles, he was thinking seriously of emigrating to Australia when Poulson's backers put their deal to him. He had nothing to lose by fighting over-matched.

The mill took place on the marshes of southern Kent, near the village of Appledore. It was a morning of hard frost, and the need to 'rough' horses against slipping on icy roads caused many spectators to miss the start. To their gratification, it proved a long slog. The disparity in weight between the men when stripped was glaring. Poulson, planted firmly on both legs, hands high in the accepted manner, looked a blockhouse. Sayers, slight by comparison, appeared casual in attitude. He came to scratch left arm low, countenance gloomy, swaying evasively. Tom Paddock, at the ringside, summed up expectations by placing 3 to 1 on his old Midlands rival.

At first, Sayers's chances of survival seemed entirely based on eluding the navvy. Only gradually did the Fancy, perceiving the astuteness of the Londoner, realize it was watching a craftsman. Wrote one reporter: 'His quickness, steadiness and judgement not only astonished his adversary and his backers, but completely surprised his friends.' His punches, deceptively effortless to the eye, jolted Poulson. Nor was Sayers lacking in wrestling skills. His closing and throwing was dexterous. When Poulson wrapped a massive arm round his opponent's neck, jabbing at his face with the free fist, Sayers pitched him to the frozen ground with a cross-buttock (a hip throw) that knocked the breath from the Midlander.

Round by round, the pattern became more evident, Poulson expending his strength in ponderous sallies: Sayers evading, conserving energy, countering crisply in controlled bursts. Repeatedly, as the battle approached its end, the flagging Poulson bored into a two-fisted battery that might have stopped a fresh fighter of less resilience. The penultimate round saw him floored for the umpteenth time. Returning 'slowly and all abroad', in the words of a witness, he missed with a despairing swing which dragged his head forward, unguarded. Sayers hit him with a right to the jaw, and the fight was done. Poulson wept on awakening to find the contest over. Only time, and the knowledge that he had met a phenomenon—a second Bendigo, as many had it—assuaged his grief.

3 Tom and Sarah

Nothing venture, nothing win—
Blood is thick, but water's thin—
In for a penny, in for a pound—
It's Love that makes the world go round!
WILLIAM SCHWENCK GILBERT

Tom Sayers, the son of a Brighton cobbler, had moved to London as a youth to lay bricks with the construction gangs building the bridges and viaducts that were to open the north of the metropolis to railway traffic. At first, he had lived in Agar's Town, a notorious slum including many of the three thousand dwellings to be demolished for St Pancras rail terminus. Here, in a maze of dank back-to-back terraces, devoid of yards and sanitation, labourers reared families on fourteen shillings a week. Women and girls earned half as much for grinding manual work. Here, as night fell, cheap lodging houses and thieves' kitchens filled with the unkempt; gas-lamps flared above drunken brawls.

Recreations for the poor of London were coarse and cheap. There were two-penny brothels, cockpits and rattings. Low-grade music halls featured lewd dances and obscene songs. Those who could afford to—and many who could not—spent their money on liquid anodynes. Consumption of alcohol in Britain was soaring towards a level estimated a few years later at almost a gallon and a half of spirits and more than thirty-four gallons of beer a year for every man, woman and child in the country. Exacerbating poverty, bringing misery and violence through drunkenness, drink addiction horrified respectable Victorians. Brewers and distillers prospered. Amid the many pubs handy to Agar's Town were the renowned Adam and Eve, on the Hampstead road, and the Green Man, on the site of the Farthing Pie House noted by

Defoe and Pope. Sayers observed the trade at such taverns with wide eyes.

Already a novice fist-fighter, Sayers could identify many well known pugilists with the sporting houses they tenanted, sometimes owned. In London, the Castle, Holborn; the Hole in the Wall, Chancery Lane; the Three Tuns, Moor Street; the Catherine Wheel, St James's Street; the Queen's Head, Windmill Street; the Union Arms, Panton Street; the Horse and Trumpeter, Aldgate; the Rising Sun, Air Street; the Nag's Head, South Audley Street; the Horseshoe, Tichbourne Street; the Coach and Horses, St Martin's Lane, among others renowned in sporting circles, were run by fighters or ex-fighters. In the provinces, bruisers' pubs were no less familiar, from the Albion, Portsmouth, to the Belt and the Molly Maloney in Liverpool. The Midlands abounded in them: the Stag's Head, Sheffield; the Three Crowns, Nottingham; the Red Lion, Appleby. There were half a dozen in Birmingham. Norwich had the Anchor and the Swan Inn; Bristol, the Guildhall Tavern. Sayers dreamed of becoming a prize-fighting publican.

By 1847, still only nineteen, he had scratched together enough capital to purchase the tenancy of the Laurel Tree, a scruffy alehouse in Bagham Street, Camden. Here he installed the woman he had taken up with. Mrs Sarah Powell was two years older than himself, and parted from her husband. To Sayers, unable to read or write, barely numerate, the ambitious Sarah seemed a queenly mate. Pretty, with a pertness he misconstrued as dignity, she possessed social aspirations. If, for his own part, he lacked polish—if his doleful features and earnest affection did not scintillate—Sayers must have seemed to Sarah at least biddable. The respect accorded his fists in the neighbourhood left no doubt he could protect her. As a bonus, there was sometimes prize-money.

But the Laurel Tree was not Sarah's dream. Bagham Street, though a cut above Agar's Town, was seedy, and the pub affronted her sensibilities. Sayers was instructed to find a home more in line with her pretensions. The result, 51 Camden Street, seemingly passing as middle-class, became the abode of their first child, another Sarah, in 1848. A second, Thomas, was born three years later. Some time afterwards Powell, the absent husband, died, allowing Sarah to marry her pugilist. The savage attitude of the day towards children born out of wedlock had weighed heavily on Sayers, and the couple had always presented themselves as married. Their wedding did not legitimize the children as the law stood, but it did regularize their birth certificates. Sarah Powell had been entered on both as Tom Sayers's spouse.

Other problems were unresolved. Sarah's standards strained a modest income. Sayers was proud of the smart clothes she wore, of the way she kept the house and dressed the infants. But funding her style of life was difficult. The Laurel Tree had failed to bear golden fruit. Neither its poky proportions nor the financial ineptitude of its host helped to capitalize Sayers's reputation in the prize-ring. In the summer of 1853, now outstanding among British middleweights, he took a gamble and opened a larger house, the Bricklayer's Arms, in near-by York Street. Prudently, he left its management to a more businesslike deputy, his brother Jack, while concentrating on his ring career. Meanwhile, Sarah augmented her extravagances. Small Sarah was sent to an expensive kindergarten. A nurse was employed to look after baby Thomas.

A new hazard was looming in the bruiser's life. Among the customers at the Bricklayer's was a smoothly personable man in his late twenties named Alfred Aldridge. Aldridge's brother, John, ran a fashionable West End gambling house at which Alfred was a croupier. Flattered by his interest in the boxing world, Sayers introduced Aldridge to 51 Camden Street, where he quickly became a familiar guest. Sayers, in turn, was introduced to 6 St James's Square, home of Aldridge's gaming rooms. Among the wealthy and indolent clients who met there, and at nearby Crockford's, the boxer was beyond his depth. 'Them toffs,' he told Jack Sayers, returning one evening to the Camden pub, 'lose more in an evening than our old man earned in a lifetime. They don't know what work is.' His liking for Aldridge waned. Lack of cash proscribed his gambling jaunts. The pub was not flourishing. Trade depended heavily on the thirst of a fickle Fancy, and the proprietor, starved at length of middleweight opponents, was slipping from the public eye. Custom drifted elsewhere.

By 1854, when he embarked on a despairing quest for a prize-match in the provinces, Sayers already faced insolvency. His wife was not the only one glad to be rid of his glum face. Alfred Aldridge's attraction to 51 Camden Street had become increasingly independent of the head of its household. For Aldridge, the neat parlour was more inviting shared simply with its mistress. Sarah did not complain. Aldridge was everything she wished her husband: suave, entertaining, sexually imaginative. When Jack Sayers arrived one evening to find the pair in his brother's bed, Sarah was unabashed. Jack hurled the croupier from the house, denouncing his sister-in-law in rough terms.

Undeterred, Sarah began visiting Aldridge at his lodgings in Pentonville, east of Camden Town. By the time Sayers returned from a futile tour, his wife's amorous trips were well established. Shamelessly, she took her stand behind the children. Young Sarah was then six. With her mother's prettiness and something of her father's enigmatic depth, she had a poise embellished by her middle-class tutorship. Thomas was 'a sturdy, open-faced lad, a chip off the old block'. They were the pride of Tom Sayers's existence, and his wife knew it. Long afterwards, the ultimatum she delivered was revealed by the Sayers family.

'Sarah said she intended to see Alfred Aldridge as and when she pleased. There was no need for the children to know, but if Tom wished to make a meal of it, they might as well know the truth about themselves, too. It was up to him. And he'd best find some money, she added. "Before you know it, they'll be off to boarding school. You can't pay for that, on top of everything, with more debts." ' Sarah's blackmail was to prove effective to the end of her husband's days— longer, as it turned out. From the start, he capitulated helplessly.

While Sarah continued to visit Aldridge and to spend what she thought fit, a façade of affection was maintained between the Sayerses for the children's sake. Financially, the outlook was darkening. Pressed by his creditors, Sayers sold the Bricklayer's Arms and talked despondently of going to Australia. For a while, bankruptcy was staved off with the help of friends. Then, when all hopes of recovery seemed misplaced, the offer from Poulson's sponsors came Sayers's way. Those who protested his madness to accept failed to see his desperation. He would he said later, have 'fought an elephant for fifty quid'.

*

The mill at Appledore won Sayers a valuable ally. John Gideon, an engaging dilettante of the *genre* popularly labelled 'man-about-town', diversified his interests between the arts, the City and the sporting world. Of the theatre and the prize-ring, he was a shrewd judge. The

Poulson fight aroused his speculative instincts. Sayers impressed Gideon as a hot tip for the champion, 'provided his personal problems could be straightened out'. These, though only vaguely known to the Fancy, suggested the need for some sound advice. John Gideon appointed himself Sayers's guide and counsellor.

By now, the pugilist was living away from Camden Street through the week, returning at weekends when the children were home from school. Even so, the charade of conjugal equanimity was a strain on him. Gideon uncovered the arrangements fortuitously. Arriving at No. 51 for a chat with his protégé, he was confronted by a withering Sarah and the news that 'Mr Sayers lives at 16 Claremont Square, Pentonville'. This, it transpired, was the address of Sayers's sister, Mary King, his landlady from Monday to Friday night. Gideon rapidly learned more. Sayers was not anxious to be lectured by his sporting friends. When the wisdom of his domestic arrangements was questioned, he clammed up. The exchange, as John Gideon recalled it, was short and blunt.

Gideon: 'By keeping up this farce of still being at one with your wife when the children are present, you may be creating trouble for them in the future, not to say for yourself now.'

Sayers: 'So long as the nippers are happy, that's all that matters. Just content yourself backing me, mister. I won't let you down.'

The next contest, with Aaron Jones, underlined the point. Jones, a clever boxer in his prime, extended Sayers in a dour two-day battle, dusk closing on an inconclusive bout the first evening. Throughout, Sayers showed remarkable nerve and endurance against a heavier opponent. Gideon, staked at 5 to 4 on the Camden man, encouraged him volubly, plying him with hot tea and brandy between rounds. It was February, the wind icy. Jones later complained he was beaten because his own corner overlooked the provision of hot drinks. Sayers shrugged off the argument. He did not, he told Gideon, rely on stimulants. Resilience was something that came to him naturally. 'My head clears. The pain goes. I feel very cool and it seems like I've exchanged my body for a new one.'

Victory over Poulson and Jones was offset by fresh domestic crises. The earlier fight preceded the death of Sayers's mother, for whom he felt particular affection. In order to be near his father, Sayers found the old man a small place in Camden and fetched his chattels from Brighton. The Jones contest was followed by drama of another kind. Gideon learned of it at Owen Swift's sporting house, the Horseshoe in Tichbourne Street. It was a lively place, cheery with polished brass, coloured prints, a sideboard of cold meats and pickled eggs. But the Sayers brothers, Tom and Jack, drank alone in gloomy ambience. Sarah was pregnant, Jack informed Gideon, by Aldridge. There had been a 'bust up', and the children knew. His views on Aldridge were not, at that time, printable.

The complications predicted by Gideon were taking shape. Sarah now demanded notice before Sayers saw the children, arranging to be out whenever he called round. At the same time, she intimated her need for an increased allowance when the third child arrived. Gideon was horrified. Both he and his solicitor, Gale of Furnival's Inn, strongly advised Sayers to divorce his wife and remove the children from her. Tom Sayers was obdurate. 'They are happier as they are,' he persisted. 'To take them from their mother would make them unhappy. I can't do it.' Had he mentioned that they were illegitimate, at least the folly of his next step might have been stopped. Instead, at Sarah's instigation, the boy born to her that winter was registered as her husband's son. Certainly, she gave him the Christian names of James Aldridge, but, in law, he was a Sayers. The croupier's son had become the pugilist's legal heir.

4 A Question of Method

In 1857, having joined the growing band of men defeated by the new 'marvel' of British boxing, the stylish heavyweight Aaron Jones left the country in disgust for America. The struggle with Sayers had taken place in appalling conditions on the bank of the Thames, near Canvey Island. To throw off the police, principals and spectators had embarked on a hired boat at Tilbury docks and sailed in the face of a head gale to the estuary before slewing round back to the Essex coast.

Rough water produced violent sea-sickness among the voyagers. The best ground which could be found on landing was soggy and uneven. It was piercingly cold, and the small body of enthusiasts which had turned out huddled round the ring like refugees from the Crimean War. To exacerbate matters, darkness fell before the battle could be resolved, and the contest was resumed on the same spot another day. After an aggregate of four or more hours in the ring, Jones was compelled to concede by the grimness of his injuries. He received eight pounds for his efforts—the proceeds of a collection made for him by his conqueror.

New York, that year, was not a joyful refuge. The economic disaster of '57 ruined more than 900 merchants, paralysed business and drove thousands into the already deep ranks of the unemployed. Urchins scavenged trash-cans in the backstreets. Restaurants emptied, their *ensembles* hard-pressed to render Strauss with a zestful lilt. So preposterous was the squalling of starving cats in the city that Cornelius

Vanderbilt hired his own exterminator, Ikey Vesuvius, in the hope of getting a night's sleep. For all of which, Jones found America more welcoming than had that earlier emissary of British pugilism, Deaf Burke.

The years between had seen prize-fighting gather force in the United States. As a free entertainment appealing chiefly to the urban proletariat, it was a diversion for men without work to do. Moreover, Aaron Jones, unusually personable for a bruiser, was an altogether more attractive ambassador than the buffoonish Burke. 'Being a fine-looking young fellow, of good address and of quiet and civil deportment,' reported one sports writer with mild surprise, 'he found much favour as a teacher of the fistic art. . . . His anecdotes of British boxers and exemplifications of the English method became fashionable among the young bloods of New York.'

So far as science could be said to have entered the prize-ring, Jones was among its best-known representatives. Perhaps lacking the instinct of a champion, he was acknowledged in fighting circles as a 'professor' of some eminence. Most theoretically minded British maulers of the fifties owed inspiration to a remarkable boxing manual published in 1841 by *Bell's Life*, the leading journal of the Fancy, and written by its editor, Francis Dowling. Dowling had spent half his life at the ringside, and was a referee of distinction. His manual, *Fistiana, or the Oracle of the Ring*, contained, among other things, 'Scientific Hints on Sparring'. As a disciple of Dowling's analytical approach, Aaron Jones commended to America the *Oracle*'s introduction to the subject:

It is frequently urged that mistaken impressions or objectionable habits may be imbibed from books; even so, the instructor is enabled by comparison and illustration to exhibit the value of the perfect over the imperfect system. . . . To excel, it must be borne in mind, a competent teacher is indispensable, therefore it is that we would recommend theory to be followed by continuous practice with a competent antagonist, especially by those who purpose boxing professionally.

Among prize-fighters, asserted Dowling, sparring—that is, fight practice with padded gloves—was as essential as sword exercise to a dragoon sergeant. It was 'the grammar of pugilistic literacy'. Indeed, Dowling prescribed sparring without qualms for a surprisingly wide sample of the human race:

> A knowledge of sparring, independent of its uses as a means of self-defence, has the additional recommendation of being one of the most healthful exercises by which the vigour of the body can be improved. The whole frame partakes of its beneficial consequences when heartily pursued; the muscular conformation is brought into beneficial action, and the latent energies of the system gradually but effectually developed. As the health of the mind is influenced by the health of the body, additional stimulants to its pursuit are offered, and as sparring can be produced at all seasons and all hours—by the old as well as by the young, by the weak as by the powerful—without danger of personal injury, we know of no sort of athletic exercise more to be commended.

In Dowling's opinion, half an hour of sparring was more beneficial to a man of sedentary occupation than two hours of walking. Whether or not Aaron Jones actually persuaded many of 'the weak' and 'the old' to set about one another at his academy is questionable, but certainly the New York fight community paid attention to his demonstrations. Reaction was mixed. Most American pugs, accustomed to depend on instinct and brute strength, were disinclined to contemplate their methods; even more so, to modify what came naturally for the sake of 'science'. On the other hand, a number of keen amateurs were impressed by the techniques of the British school. Some, involved as punters and sponsors with the prize-ring, could influence its combatants.

An impression of 'the English method' of the period may be gained from the *Oracle*. Much stress was placed on the way a fighter shaped up.

> The body should be equally poised, the feet about twenty inches apart, the left in advance pointing to your adversary, the right a little back and firmly planted for a spring forward or backward. The head should be well up, and the arms in advance, the right more forward than the left and sufficiently high to embrace freedom of action, while the chest, with full front, is well covered. . . .

The hands should not be closed tightly before you mean to hit, but that resolved upon they should be clenched firmly and sent forth as a solid mass of bone, the full front of the knuckles in advance in as straight a line as possible to the point of contact. . . . Your left toe and knee should invariably be pointed to your adversary, for in their direction will your blow inevitably go. Some men in hitting with the left, or *vice versa*, throw up the other hand to guard the head. This is decidedly bad, diminishing the intended delivery of one half of its force, besides interfering with a clear view of the adversary. . . .The right hand, in our opinion, ought always to be used in reserve, to guard the head or body, while the left is used for execution.

According to Dowling, the best 'modern' fighters aimed primarily at the face, particularly the nose 'as its contusion affects both eyes and prevents effective delivery. The eyes are not less important to assail.' Body blows, he considered, were most effective against a tiring or slow opponent. Counter-hitting—that is, delivering with the same hand at the same time as an opponent—was 'much in vogue and, when well judged, generally tells severely'. Sharing the preference of most spectators for an attacking fighter, the *Oracle* encouraged a positive mental outlook:

No man can expect to win a battle without the chance of punishment; regardless, therefore, of consequences to yourself, although fully prepared to stop a like game, forthwith make play, let fly smack with your left at the first glimpse of an opening, darting into action resolved to conquer or die. It is not impossible that this very display of fearless confidence will gain vantage ground which you may preserve throughout the fight. Whenever you hit, however, take care the steam is well up, and that determination of body and mind go hand in hand: no half-measures will do.

Enemy blows in the prize-ring were deflected by the forearm. The *Oracle* described methods of stopping punches at head and body.

In stopping a coming blow at the head, the right elbow should be raised and the arm turned as if you were lifting a glass of wine to the mouth. By this means, the muscular part of the arm is presented to the shock, and, by a quick action of the forearm at the moment of contact, the blow is thrown off. With a dead stop, not only might the muscle of your arm be injured, but even the bone broken. . . . To stop a body blow, you have only to drop your right elbow close to the side with your forearm on the chest. This should be followed by a dab from your left.

The technique of in-fighting, with wrestling holds, exercised the theorists. A closing opponent, according to Dowling, 'will have one of two objects in view—to seize you with one hand and fib [*short-punch*] with the other, or to get you in such a position as to give you a fall. This is easier fancied than done, and while he is trying to grasp you with one hand, and to hit with the other, keep both your arms disengaged and counter with short-armed blows till wrestling becomes inevitable. Then if, as you ought, you know anything of the use of your legs, you will give him a crook, with a cant or good backfall.' The *Oracle* did not flinch from tortuous wrestling tips.

If by chance you are lucky enough to get your left or right arm over your adversary's neck, with his head under your arm, while his arm is round your waist, do not fail with the other hand to give him an upper-cut. If you can secure his disengaged arm by crooking your own, which is over his neck, under it (the so-called Suit in Chancery) the punishment to him will be awful. If you happen yourself to get into this position, shift your outside hand up to his face and force his head back as a twitch would the head of a vicious horse.

Another trick with an opponent in a neck hold was to cant him over the hip or buttock—hence 'cross buttock'—hurling him on his back. 'If well done, he goes over with tremendous violence, and you fall on his abdomen. The chances are that he is either rendered insensible or stupified by the double concussion.'

To what extent Jones, in his coaching, refined the gospel of Dowling is unknown. The tactics of evasion and stalking were not approved in the *Oracle*. Its purport was to produce the blood and guts spectacle approved by the fight crowds, not a display of manœuvring. 'To the modern development of long sparring and getting away, we have a strong objection: it is tedious and fruitless.' Yet it was partly just such a development, enabling lighter fighters to live with the big men, that had allowed Bendigo to reach the summit, and was helping Sayers to the same heights. Jones himself was a long-shooter, inclined to play possum. In all, it may be said with fair safety, he showed his audience in New York something of the more 'educated' aspects of English pugilism.

★

Most Americans thought of a prize-fighter in the fifties as a natural spoiler, a pugnacious roughneck who, like John Morrissey, alleged national champion, had little time for theory or instruction. Morrissey, a huge, flamboyant figure later prominent as a gambler and crude politician, was already a password for violence in New York by '57. Men told how his first exploit on reaching the city from the Hudson, where he had worked as a deckhand on a steamboat, had been to invade Dutch Charley's sporting saloon, the Empire Club, and challenge all present to combat. Seemingly, the beating he received diminished neither his swagger nor his belligerence.

Back-street ragamuffins who scarcely knew Lincoln from the local rat-catcher could give chapter and verse for the bear-like Morrissey's rumbustious history. Son of destitute immigrants from Tipperary, Ireland, he had learned the rudiments of brawling as a child in Troy, New York State, his adoptive home. There, he roamed the streets wild while his father looked in vain for work. In 1848, aged seventeen, Morrissey joined Captain Eli Smith's crew on the Hudson, conceiving the audacious ambition to possess the captain's daughter. Later, he actually married her. Meanwhile, his early days in New York saw him touting for a sleazy dockland boarding-house. His job, to drum business among newly landed immigrants, led to skirmishes with rival 'runners', and his sobriquet 'Old Smokey'.

It appears that another tout, Tom McCann, resenting Morrissey's intrusion, held him against a barrel-stove of glowing coals until the clothes on his back were in cinders. Morrissey broke free and beat McCann senseless. Already, he was flirting with the professional ring, but the promise of quicker riches delayed his prize-fight career. Lured west in the California gold scramble, Morrissey bummed vainly across the continent, to return as poor as he set out. His only hope of recognition now lay in hammering a path to the top with his knuckles, and, on 12 October 1853, he succeeded to the extent of vanquishing James Ambrose at Boston Four Corners. If anyone had been in doubt about Ambrose's title, Morrissey made his own clear to all who valued their ribs and teeth: he was the U.S. champion and the toast of New York.

Embarking on a turbulent programme of gambling, saloon-keeping and labour manipulation, Morrissey acquired many enemies. He could be generous as well as unscrupulous, but his methods had always been bare-fisted, and many who bore bruises did not forget. Among them, one group sought satisfaction where the hurt to his prestige would be greatest: in the prize-ring. The tool of their vengeance was a superb young athlete, formerly a foundryman, whose strong-arm services in recent elections had earned him a sinecure in the New York customs office. All he needed to whip 'Old Smokey', as the syndicate saw it, were a few scientific hints. Aaron Jones was commissioned to advise on training John C. Heenan.

5 A Bit of a Snapping Turtle

Have you heard of Philip Slingsby,
Him of the manly chest;
How he slew the Snapping Turtle
In the regions of the West?
WILLIAM E. AYTOUN

'Professor' Jones contemplated his student with interest. John Carmel
Heenan weighed thirteen stone eight pounds, and stood just under six
feet two inches. Broad shoulders, narrow hips and a handsome,
smoothly groomed head gave him an unmistakably athletic appearance.
'His frame was a model for a sculptor. Every muscle was developed,
every tendon and sinew visible. It is doubtful if such a Herculean
specimen had been seen in the prize-ring for many years.' Heenan, then
twenty-two, had perfected his physique in the foundries of the Pacific
Mail Steamship Company, at Benicia, California, where he had thrown
a thirty-two pound sledge twelve hours a day, fighting the local
favourites at weekends for extra cash. Apart from some want of
'science', which Jones guaranteed to rectify, the 'Benicia Boy', as
Heenan's backers dubbed their man, seemed a sound bet.

If there was a doubt about the 'Boy', it was his temperament. Easy-
going and amiable, Heenan preferred togging up and making friends,
particularly women friends, to stripping down and fighting. He was
not, as was Morrissey, essentially aggressive. His strength had led him
to exploit his arm in the ring and mob politics, but the soft billet he now
occupied in the customs service was more to his liking. Despite the
urging of Morrissey's enemies, who produced 2,500 dollars to stake
Heenan, he consented reluctantly to the fight. One factor in his decision
was his old Benicia mentor and manager, Jim Cusick, a small bustling
man with boundless energy and faith in the young pugilist. Cusick's

faith had brought him to New York with Heenan. It overcame the resentment he felt at the supervisory appointment of Aaron Jones. Heenan agreed to fight more for Cusick's sake than his own gain.

Cusick was sceptical about Jones's ability. 'The Boy doesn't need any goddam English tricks,' he told a friend. But it seems indubitable that Heenan benefited from the pro's advice. Reports spoke of skills the 'Boy' was unlikely to have picked up as a wage-packet mauler in the far west. 'Heenan,' declared the *New York Times*, 'was the more scientific of the combatants, Morrissey being an extremely uncultivated fighter.' Moreover, both Heenan and Cusick later talked of Jones with improved respect. At all events, it was certainly not the fault of Aaron Jones that Heenan failed to consummate the best hopes of 'Old Smokey's' foes. To their discomfort, Heenan took ill during training and contested the fight in poor condition—'hog fat', as one writer overstated it.

The battle took place on 20 October 1858, at Long Point, Canada, across the lake from Erie, Pennsylvania, to avoid the attention of the U.S. sheriffs. Against the possibility of Canadian intervention, the ring was pitched on the beach beneath Long Point lighthouse, a chartered steamer standing close for a getaway. For the most part, the spectators comprised the New York mobs of Morrissey and his rivals. 'A worse set of scapegallowses,' wrote a contemporary journalist, 'could scarcely be collected; low, filthy, brutal, bludgeon-bearing scoundrels—the very class of men who have built up the Tammany Hall party in New York and to whose well-paid labours the party owes almost its existence.' Morrissey, twelve stone seven pounds, fit and scowling, was well aware the fight owed little to the spirit of sportsmanship.

From the first, Heenan's superiority in boxing skill was evident. Morrissey, swinging crudely, missed repeatedly in the opening round, while Heenan, finding the face with effective shots, forced his man to the ropes and belaboured him. When Morrissey attempted a bear-hug, the 'Boy' broke it convincingly, placed a leg behind the champion and deftly threw him. The contest progressed in Heenan's favour for several rounds. Morrissey looked clumsy and set for a beating. Noted the *New York Times* cryptically: 'Heenan's left twice on Morrissey's nose and eye, drawing claret. Morrissey badly punished. Heenan's blows terrific. Morrissey unable to equal the hits of the Benicia Boy.

Morrissey down again.' The champion's friends, led by one Patrick Mulligan, had begun to seethe. While Mulligan roared 'Foul!' whenever Heenan scored heavily, the more astute of the champion's supporters, perceiving the challenger's surplus flesh, urged their favourite to go for the body.

At last, as a barrage from Heenan found the head again, Morrissey aimed desperately for Heenan's kidneys. The reaction was significant. Heenan was still struggling for breath when Morrissey threw him and fell on him. The 'Boy' came back feebly, hands low, and Morrissey repeated the formula. Charging forward, he threw the challenger a second time, pitching on his belly with vengeful force. An abrupt rise in the champion's stock—originally evens, now 10 to 6—testified to the slump in Heenan's prospects. Worse awaited him. Blowing painfully, he threw an ill-judged hook, struck a stake, and damaged his left fist. No takers at 10 to 2.

Heenan handled his handicap creditably. In the sixth round, he shook Morrissey with a flurry of counters; in the ninth, he took the fight to the enemy. But his strength was spent against a foe who, though bloody, still possessed stamina. Roared on by Mulligan and his cronies, Morrissey hammered the lower half of his opponent's trunk, dropping on it when the younger man hit the ground. 'Both combatants came up tired for the eleventh,' the *New York Times* recorded, 'but Heenan the more so. The striking was in favour of Morrissey. On Heenan aiming and missing, Morrissey put in a huge blow on the jugular. Heenan fell on his face. The champion stepped away from him. Heenan could not make time.' Morrissey had saved his title.

Little else could be granted him, except his dogged pluck. The most fervent of his partisans knew that Heenan must have triumphed but for bad luck. Even now, he looked the winner, being virtually unscarred. So severely was Morrissey disfigured, by contrast, that the beard he subsequently affected was supposedly grown to hide his injuries. The lengths to which he was to go for revenge betrayed his bitterness. Meanwhile, Heenan returned to New York to find himself the idol of the sporting crowd. Unanimously, the press declared him superior in fighting skill to Morrissey. His was the 'moral victory', as one writer had it, 'endorsed by public sentiment'. The outcome was ironic. Not only was he fêted like a champion but, on the disgruntled Morrissey's announcing his retirement, Heenan was widely regarded as no less. That his fight career consisted of a single contest of note, a defeat to boot, was overlooked. New York liked John Heenan.

For a bruiser, he was singularly debonair. Tall and wide, with a dashing smile, bespoke suit and derby, the 'Boy' combined high spirits and modest charm in popular proportions. Unlike Morrissey, he was American-born of solid artisan lineage, his father foreman at a government arsenal. For many who aspired to it, if not all who possessed it, Heenan had 'style'. An English journalist thought him 'too much a gentleman' for a pugilist. At least one gentleman, on the other hand, considered him 'deficient in chivalry', unrefined and profligate. 'Anybody could impose on his feelings,' an admirer wrote. 'He was as impressionable as a twelve-year-old.' At all events, Heenan enjoyed his role. No longer the unwilling contender, he waited to prove his worth.

Cusick was exuberant. 'He fought Morrissey one-handed,' he told the doyen of the New York boxing press, George Wilkes. 'The Boy can beat anyone. He's got the muscle of a wagon-horse.' Inspired perhaps by the analogy, Heenan laughingly described himself as 'half-horse, half-alligator, and a bit of a snapping turtle'. The problem was to find an equally formidable hybrid. As Cusick recognized, matching the accepted champion with a run-of-the-mill bruiser could only diminish the 'Boy's' prestige. Anticlimax was professional death. It was Aaron Jones who struck the keynote. Jones talked a lot about the prize-ring in England, arousing interest among his New Yorker friends. If Heenan really wanted to make news, why not an invasion of the old land to carry off the British belt? It would be the supreme stroke.

Heenan, at first awed by the prospect, warmed to it. Jones spoke of Sayers, the man to beat, as an over-rated fighter. Indeed, still vexed by the failure of his own bid, the 'professor' had more than once threatened 'to return and have another shy for the belt myself'. His gossip encouraged the Heenan camp. Wilkes, consulted on procedure, agreed to contact the British press. When he asked if backers could be found for a campaign in England, Cusick was confident. 'Fighting them off will be harder than whipping Sayers,' he prophesied.

*

A few weeks after the battle at Long Point, Adah Menken arrived in New York for the first time. *Mazeppa* had yet to assure her fame. She was twenty-three, a vivacious but still obscure trouper. An inch or two above five feet in height, fluctuating in weight between eight and eight and a half stone, she possessed a pert oval face and a stature too stocky to be elegant. Though an acquaintance of her early days, authoress Celia Logan, described her as 'one of the most peerless beauties ever to dazzle human eyes', portraits confound the extravagance. Menken's appeal was strongly sexual. Full-breasted, with trim waist and ankles, she heightened her physical impact with bold make-up and manners most women of the day would have found brash. Men responded appreciatively.

But, to date, her few victories had been modest ones. Behind lay a series of small-town engagements, tawdry rooming-houses and cheap meals which must have disillusioned any but the most obsessive of careerists. Repeatedly faced with destitution, Menken had turned, when dramatic parts eluded her, to dancing, circus work, even modelling for sculptors. Her most drastic resort, by all accounts, was marriage. In a moment of weakness early in 1856, she had wed at Livingstone, Texas, one Alexander Menken, son of a Cincinnati dry-goods merchant, resigning herself to a wifely role.

It lasted little longer than her professional engagements. As her husband's conventional parents had suspected from the outset, Menken was more than usually miscast. Their first sight of her had been traumatic. 'Never,' wrote Celia Logan, who was present, 'shall I forget the hush which fell as she appeared in the doorway.' Endlessly cigarette-smoking, hankering for the acclaim she saw as her due right, Menken plainly lacked the attributes of a submissive spouse. Her moods were capricious, ranging swiftly from childlike delight to fury and cold contempt. 'The one certain prognostication,' wrote a chronicler of her passions, 'was that never would two hours with her be alike.' Eventually, in a characteristic fit of temper, Menken had stormed out from her first husband, retaining from the interlude only her married name.

New York, recovering from economic crisis, was a daunting Mecca for a friendless fortune-hunter. Behind the prim façade of well-to-do society stretched a web of administrative corruption and gaudy vice into which the unprotected could quickly fall. Union Square and the prosperous residential avenues were not hospitable to impecunious visitors. Gentlemen on horseback, swinging idly round newly purchased Central Park, cast few smiles on those without social hallmarks. To the bosses and their henchmen, the flood of immigrants spreading poverty and unemployment in the city was no more than an exploitable labour pool. From the rougher elements came the bully gangs deployed in the interests of boss rule. Whitelaw Reid, then a youthful post-graduate, had already deplored 'the wickedness of this great city'. It had, wrote Reid, produced an effect on him 'which I think time cannot ever efface'.

If Menken was less susceptible to a social conscience, she soon discovered that the sidewalks were hard and cold. In New York, unlike Livingstone, her boldness was not unique. On East Fourteenth Street, West Twenty-third Street, and elsewhere, the sounds of revelry from gambling palaces and flash saloons indicated the company of brash females by the score: 'the choicest assortment of girls in the universe'. Theatre managers kept comprehensive lists of so-called 'stars' all too ready to scramble for stage parts. Lesser hopefuls were too numerous even to have their names booked. Many were as alluring as Menken; most, more biddable. Direct assault on the impresarios of New York was futile.

Menken switched her sights astutely to the city press. The cultivation of journalists, to become a staple of her stock-in-trade, produced benefits from the start. Beneath its protective crust, she perceived, the species was vulnerable. Badgered, over-worked, disparaged by the world at large, the journalist was peculiarly open to flattery. Menken, the frustrated writer, supplied it with instinctive flair. Her esteem for men of letters came naturally. Among the first to succumb were Frank. L. Queen, editor of the influential stage paper, the *New York Clipper*, and his deputy.

Queen, good-hearted and avuncular, became her instant champion. When she needed help, his proof-littered office was her first resort. He made no bones about his partiality. 'She came to this city friendless,' wrote Queen in an open appeal to the New York press, 'with nothing to rely on but her energetic spirit . . . assist her in her efforts to support herself in a legitimate calling.' If Queen's protection was a tactical victory for Menken, her conquest of his editorial lieutenant proved a strategic triumph. Edwin James, a slick journalist with an eye for commercial perks, had considerable gifts as a promoter. Throughout what was to become the most enduring of all Menken's friendships—the more remarkable for its platonic character—James never ceased to puff her qualities in New York.

For the moment, it was neither Menken's manœuvres nor her admirers which failed her, but her patent shortcomings as an actress. In the judgement of one who knew her, she attacked 'everything in tragedy and comedy with a reckless disregard of consequences'. Actor James Murdoch recalled a drama in which, having delivered a frenzied performance in the first act, Menken completely forgot her part. 'For the rest, I gave the lady the words! Clinging to my side in a manner very different from her former bearing, she took them line by line before she uttered them.' The management promptly withdrew the play.

Now, bolstered by her influence with the press, Menken obtained her first booking in New York—to play the widow in a piece called *The Soldier's Daughter*. The notices maddened her. Whatever their private feelings for the volatile southerner, the critics were not prepared to commit professional perjury. The most obliging said the least. The best Horace Greeley's *New York Tribune* could manage was the mild reproof that Adah Menken needed 'taming down'. As usual in a crisis, she ran to the *Clipper*. James was in his office talking to a self-assured young man whose grin did nothing to calm her rage. Worse, they were discussing boxing. Moving, as did Menken, in predominantly male company, it was impossible to miss the enthusiasm for sport in New York. Even the *Clipper* was generous with sports news, much of it contributed by Edwin James. At the best of times, it provoked jealous resentment in Menken.

At that moment, she blew up. In a display of the temper that later terrified theatrical managers—they called her 'Little Tiger'—Menken delivered a tirade on the infamy of stage-hands, newspapermen, and all other heretics who rated pugilists above gifted actresses. James looked sheepish, but the man with him laughed approvingly. 'That's as true as I'm sitting here!' exclaimed Heenan. 'And I vote that we drink to it.' Not long afterwards, he asked Menken to marry him.

6 Three Battles

The pre-eminent fight chronicler of mid-Victorian Britain was Henry Downes Miles, a hearty tweed-clad Englishman who probably clambered more fences, scrambled more ditches and braved more mud to report the events of the prize-ring than even the redoubtable Francis Dowling. Apprenticed on *Bell's Life in London* under its founder Vincent G. Dowling, Miles wrote boxing pieces for many papers and periodicals, including the *Morning Advertiser* and *Sportsman's Magazine*, becoming editor of the latter. Like the Dowlings he adopted a bitter tone against the ring's opponents—'crusaders of cant, hypocrisy and cowardice . . . penny saints'—but his reports of fights and fighters were always genial. A boyish naïvety characterized his writing, in which battered bruisers were portrayed as carefree gallants, heroes all, embarking blithely on battles, suffering knocks with smiles, emerging in the spirit of true, if bloody, brotherhood.

In style, Miles borrowed something of the colloquialistic dash of Pierce Egan while labouring a more formal education. The anatomical detail of his reports was peppered with 'peepers', 'pins', 'knobs' and 'smellers'. Pugilists were prone to shed 'the claret', or 'the ruby'. At the same time, it might be believed from reading him that the rowdies of the Fancy could be inspired by Ovid or Thucydides. In the first paragraph of a report on Tom Sayers, Miles contrived to include three Latin phrases and a reference to Homer. Strong on *insouciant* bravery, Miles, with most other sports writers, skated swiftly round the misery and anguish which attended the careers of those he wrote about. This was conspicuous in his treatment of Sayers, 'the merry Tom', as Miles was apt to have him, a fighter whose haunted features, even in success, conveyed the stresses of a hard life.

Miles took up Sayers in earnest after the defeat of Aaron Jones. Suddenly the neglected Camden fighter had become, in the jargon of the journals, a giant killer, an eleven-stone wonder challenging the 'heavies' for the new belt. 'The star of Tom Sayers has rapidly arisen,' declared Miles. 'Having polished off the middleweights, he has been playing havoc among the big'un's ... Tom's triumphant *coup d'essai* with two heavyweights [*Poulson and Jones*] gives him an open view of the goal of his ambition, the Championship.'

By that year, 1857, Broome, the sometime champion from Birmingham, had retired from contention. Two British heavyweights stood within sight of supremacy. William Perry, the Potteries veteran, was thirty-eight, resolved on an autumnal triumph. Twenty years a name in the fighting world, the 'Tipton Slasher'—now more aptly dubbed 'Th' Ould Tipton'—was still calling a living at Black Country races, fairs and other outings, where he sold pies and drinks from a canvas stall. His customers, apprising the fourteen stone six pounds of sinew beneath his flat, close-cropped head, did not doubt that the big fellow was still a force. Less tested, if less time-worn, the rustic Tom Paddock awaited his moment, content that his renowned Midlands compatriot should deal with Sayers.

The Sayers–Perry match, agreed for £400 soon after the defeat of Jones, created more excitement in England than any contest since Caunt had fought Bendigo. As then, public interest centred on the disparity of size between the two men. In Poulson and Jones, the Camden fighter had despatched considerably larger opponents, but Perry was both bigger and more experienced than either. 'The matter at issue,' summarized Henry Miles, 'was whether a man of 5 feet 8½ inches, and under 11 stone—possessed of whatever science he might ·be—could contest with any chance of success against one topping 6 feet and weighing not less than 14 stone.' General opinion held the answer to be negative. Sayers, it was felt, had succumbed to bravado. Many predicted his withdrawal and forfeit before the day.

In fact, Sayers was too heavily committed to pull out. His last two victories had cleared his debts with a small amount over. Unknown to the public, the moment the match was made with Perry he had backed himself with almost every penny of the residue. Gideon had also taken advantage of the 6 to 4 odds against Sayers. He exuded quiet optimism. 'From first to last,' reported the sporting press, 'the friends of Sayers maintained that the Slasher was stale, devoid of science, and too slow.'

Miles interviewed both fighters before the battle. 'Tom intimated that he believed the Slasher was worn-out and incapable of prolonged exertion. He had made up his mind, he said, to keep him on his pins and lead him about the ring until he should be so exhausted as to be nearer his own mark.' Perry on the other hand, assured Miles that 'he had made up his mind not to run all over the ring after his opponent, but to take his stand at scratch and await the onslaughts of Sayers'. If there was a hint of self-deception in either camp, it came from Perry's side. 'The Slasher laughed at the idea of defeat, stating his firm belief that, in addition to his other advantages, he would be found the cleverer of the two.'

On 16 June, a fine day in 1857, pugilists, officials and spectators assembled at Southend to embark by steamer for an undeclared destination on the coast of Kent. With two hundred passengers aboard, the vessel left the pier and stood south for the Medway. Its progress, contrary to intention, was conspicuous. A number of excursionists, left behind by the steamer, hired alternative vessels. Other craft in the estuary, drawn by the procession, fell in behind until the unwitting flagship was heading a regular pleasure fleet. By the time it reached shore, the suspicions of the Kent constabulary matched those of the herons in the sedges. The ring was made, the fighters stripping, when the approach of blue uniforms stampeded the crowd back to the waiting boats.

Many people, in their panic, got into the wrong vessels, which at first floated aimlessly offshore. Then, on the purposeful departure of the steamer, the fleet reformed and headed for a new destination. Miles, bowler awry, trousers drenched, viewed the scene from the flagship. 'The movements of the steamer had put all the frequenters of the river on the *qui vive*, and the water was studded with boats and sailing vessels of various sizes conveying their freights to the action.' Leaving the police to summon a pursuit craft, the Fancy headed for an island, the Isle of Grain, a few miles from the first landing. Again the ring was assembled. The colours were tied to the stakes: blue and white spot for Sayers, blue birdseye for Perry. The crowd had grown to several thousand. At 4.30 p.m., the combatants finally toed the scratch.

Perry's tall frame and muscular limbs seemed in good shape, but two decades of buffeting had left their impress on his features. One spectator judged him 'on the shady side of forty'. The odds against Sayers shortened. Ringside betting was 6 to 5 on the bigger man. The crowd, largely non-partisan, was orderly. It witnessed a disciplined campaign, as planned, by Sayers, but a prompt abandonment of preconceived tactics by Perry who, from the start, went after his opponent, arms flailing. The first round ended quickly, Sayers stumbling to the ground while back-tracking. The second, sustained for almost thirty minutes, showed his technical mastery. Throughout a constant offensive by Perry, the Camden fighter avoided punishment, intermittently sniping with sharp effect. Miles described the action in characteristic prose:

[Sayers stopped Perry's initial rush with a shot to the mouth which drew first blood.] The Slasher looked astonished, stopped to consider a moment, and again went in swinging his arms like the sails of a windmill. Tom danced lightly out of harm's way, then, stepping in, popped a tidy smack on the spectacle-beam and got away laughing. After dancing round his man, easily avoiding several more lunges, Tom again got home on the snuffer-tray, removing a piece of the japan and drawing a fresh supply of the ruby. The Tipton, annoyed, rushed in, missing with his right and a terrific left upper-cut, and Sayers again dropped in upon the nose. . . . The Slasher now chased Sayers all over the ring, the latter dancing round him like a Red Indian, or fleeing like a deer, to draw him after him.

The vicious blows aimed by the Slasher all fell upon the air, his exertions to catch his nimble antagonist causing him to blow off steam to an inordinate extent. Had one of the intended compliments alighted upon Tom, it looked as if it would have been all over with him. After Sayers had completed his dance, he went to his man, cleverly avoided a good right-hander, and delivered another hot one on the proboscis—more '*Lafitte*' of the *premier crû*. The Tipton tried his heavy punches again three times and missed; a fourth attempt was prettily stopped . . . some pretty stopping followed on both sides, after which the Tipton made another rush like a bull at a gate, to find himself once more battling with vacancy. . . . The Slasher looked astonished and shook his nut.

Five rounds ended with tactical falls by Sayers. The sixth marked the watershed. Savage with frustration, increasingly leaden, Perry retired to snatch a drink and wipe a gashed cheek. Sayers was now stopping his deliveries with seeming ease. For the first time, Perry closed a round by dropping. In the seventh, he took severe punishment. Gradually, the fight was becoming a display by Sayers of systematic, coolly measured destruction. In the eighth round, Perry stood blowing, at his wits' end to defend himself. He came out slowly for the ninth, staggering as Sayers hammered his damaged face. The euphemisms of contemporary ring reporting veil the agony, but Miles conceded that Perry's appearance was 'piteous'. Somehow he survived until the eleventh round. His left eye was a blind lump; his right cheek mangled. A torn lower lip hung grotesquely from his gaping mouth. Ninety-five minutes had elapsed since the fight began. Belatedly, Perry's corner tossed in the sponge.

By now, the Kent police had obtained a boat and were approaching the island at full speed. Again, there was a rush from the ring to the waiting fleet, some components of which departed with indecent haste. One charter vessel, the *Widgeon*, steamed away leaving the majority of her passengers stranded. Aboard the flagship, consultation among the fight organizers produced a decision to run up the Medway for Strood, Kent, rather than attempt to evade the police in the estuary. Wearily, the pugilists and their supporters disembarked at that town at 11 p.m., to find lodgings or trek through the night towards London. For Perry, it was a dismal end to a long career. A collection made for him on the steamer raised twenty-two pounds and five shillings.

*

Before the 'railway mania' of the forties, fight enthusiasts had travelled to battles in England by foot, horse-cab or stage coach. Sport correspondents covered the country by courtesy of such notable mail outfits as the *High Flyer*, the *Age*, and the *Red Rover* of the Brighton road. It was tiring, a long-winded process, vulnerable to interception by the law. Railroads revolutionized prize-fight logistics. Special excursion trains could now speed thousands of supporters from the cities to remote rural locations—and home again—in a few hours, catching the local authorities unprepared. Increasingly, the railway companies featured in the sporting scene. The main alternative was water transport. This appealed in particular to Londoners, served by a regular fleet of river steamers, including the *Queen of the Thames*, the *City of Rochester*, the *Nelson* and the Woolwich *Nymph*. By charter vessel, the empty marshes below Greenhithe, or the police-free islands of the estuary, were quickly reached.

Six months after the Perry fight, Sayers returned to the Isle of Grain to dispose of an unexpected challenge. Tom Paddock, seemingly the one man left to dispute possession of the champion's belt, had contracted rheumatic fever. The prognosis was not good. In his place, an obscure Gloucestershire brawler, William Bainge (alias Benjamin) of Northleach, claimed the right to a match by staking the conditional two hundred pounds. Bainge was something of a mystery. A twelve-stoner of strong physique, his form was parochial. The press reckoned him a novice. Yet his sponsors included the veteran Harry Broome and a canny trainer and professional gambler named Massey. Jemmy Massey was known to have backed the outsider heavily. Talk of a conspiracy involving Sayers, though disputed by those who knew him, became fashionable.

Sayers, as Gideon knew, could be difficult. His contrariness and truculence sometimes upset patrons accustomed to deference from mere pugs. But of his integrity, friends had no doubt. He was deeply offended by the gossip. When the day came, the men walked to the scratch amid unusual silence from a puzzled crowd. Broome and Massey, in Bainge's corner, seemed confident. Their fighter, the more powerful-looking man, shaped up stylishly. His opening prods and feints appeared businesslike. Sayers stood motionless. His doleful features were inscrutable, but his eyes had a nasty glint. The idle defamation of Sayers's character had done Bainge a poor service. As the Gloucestershire man attempted his first punch, Sayers hit him in the belly with vicious force, then hammered his jaw as he buckled. Dragged to his corner, Bainge blinked with disbelief.

He came out for the second apprehensively, as if his mind was settled on early flight. Walking quietly up to him, Sayers flighted a single ranging shot before launching a left which knocked his antagonist off his feet. Bainge lay prone for a moment, then sat up and held his head. Half lifted, half pulled aside by his seconds, he appeared indifferent to their advice. Massey's face darkened. Gesturing disgustedly, he turned his back and left the ring. Broome manhandled Bainge forward for the third round. It was effort wasted. Almost instantly, he was down again, this time decisively. The contest lasted six minutes.

By the beginning of '58, Paddock had arisen from his sickbed and, being destitute, returned to the ring against sound counsel. His old sponsors were discouraging. Few believed his protestations of recovery, and it was with difficulty that he raised the stake to challenge Sayers. After narrowly eluding police pursuit, the contestants came to grips on Canvey Island on 16 June, the anniversary of the Sayers–Perry fight. It was a hot day and Paddock, normally florid, was highly flushed. The first round, of fifteen minutes, convinced many, including Paddock, of the outcome. Already, he was sweating profusely and had retreated to his corner to cool off. Afterwards, the ubiquitous Henry Miles, himself 'sticky at the collar', heard from Paddock that he had lost hope by the end of the quarter-hour. That he persevered, nevertheless, for a gruelling eighty minutes, mostly worsted in the exchanges and distressingly damaged, was proof of his sore economic straits.

The only real likelihood of a verdict against Sayers, on a foul, was pursued by Paddock's seconds with remorseless zeal. In the thirteenth round, when Sayers slipped and fell as Paddock lunged at him, they stormed from the corner claiming an intended dive. Many of Paddock's less reputable backers took cause with them, and for some time the referee was menaced by a swearing and jostling mob. Miles, who held a gentleman's view of such behaviour, was gratified when the ring-whips waded into the 'blackguards'. In the seventeenth round, a complaint was made that Sayers had deliberately spiked Paddock, who indeed sustained two lesions on the leg. Again, in the nineteenth, Paddock's seconds protested, this time that their man had been kneed in the stomach. But the guards protected the referee from more assaults.

Two rounds later, the contest was over. Groggy and half-blind, Paddock stumbled to the scratch for the twenty-first occasion, bravely attempting another rush. Sayers side-stepped and caught him on the right cheek. Paddock staggered. Seeing him grope semi-consciously for support, Sayers grasped him firmly and led him to his corner. The Redditch farm-hand made one more appearance in a prize-ring. In 1860, he was defeated in nine and a half minutes by Sam Hurst, a cumbersome wrestler whose boxing pretensions were moderate. Paddock had never recovered his health. He died three years later after a lingering illness. Meanwhile, by the end of '58, Sayers's claim to the belt was undisputed in Britain. It remained for America to take up the challenge.

7 View Halloo!

The dusky night rides down the sky,
And ushers in the morn;
The hounds all join in glorious cry,
The huntsman winds his horn:
And a-hunting we will go.
HENRY FIELDING

The first intimation of an American challenge for the belt to reach England arrived in the form of a letter on the desk of Francis Dowling at *Bell's Life*, 5 Norfolk Street, Strand, London. It was a bitter March morning. A coal fire crackled in the front room, the editorial sanctum where, in their time, cabinet ministers and knights—sporting patrons of real influence—had sat to discuss pugilism with the editor. As the premier medium of boxing news in the nation, *Bell's Life* had long enjoyed quasi-bureaucratic status within the Fancy. The tradition was important to Dowling, who tackled his duties earnestly. Unlike Miles, he projected a certain formality. A tale relished among journalists related how a yokel, spotting Dowling's top hat and frock coat at a provincial fight, once exclaimed: 'That's editor of *Bell's Loife*? Damme if I didn't take 'un for a gentleman!'

Pocketing the American letter, Dowling pulled on his overcoat and went into the narrow road. A north wind blew toward the Thames. He turned into the teeth of it. At the corner, opposite Aldwych, where a one-armed victim of the Crimean War held out his cap for coins, Dowling wheeled left, proceeding west on the river side of 'the first street of Europe'. In the spacious Strand, with its impressive buildings and multi-paned windows loaded with merchandise, the shopping might have been led on a warmer occasion by such ladies of the carriage trade as the gracious Lady Palmerston; the ageing, painted

Mrs Disraeli; Jane Carlyle in her pretty one-horse brougham. That day, women who patronized select shops were by their firesides embroidering in antimacassared comfort.

Occupants of the coaches that whirled past Dowling were thickly rugged. Creaking and rattling, a stream of more mundane vehicles used the Strand: hansoms, horse-buses, trade wagons and heavy drays. At intervals, road-sweepers advanced to clear the horse-dung, while urchins turned cartwheels for pennies. At the corner of Adam Street, Dowling entered Osborne's Hotel, where John Gideon would be waiting. Osborne's (later, the Adelphi) had many literary and sporting associations. Gibbon had stayed there on completing *Decline and Fall*; the cartoonist Rowlandson had died there; the hotel figured prominently in *The Pickwick Papers*. Americans liked to stay at Osborne's.

Sport and the arts had yet to be torn apart. At a time when even 'respectable' theatre was strictly popular—the classics were 'brightened'; domestic drama was stagey and sensational—the dual preoccupation of such as Gideon and Edwin James with the theatre and prize-ring was not deemed incongruous. Indeed, the two activities shared a rare distinction, being among the few aspects of Victorian life devoid of class exclusiveness. Thick-eared bruisers were as at home in the audience at the Theatre Royal as were Gideon's theatrical friends at a knuckle-fight. There was even a temperamental affinity. Gideon's attachment to the prize-ring, particularly to Sayers, had a sentimental side any stage artist would have recognized. Among his most cherished possessions was a pair of the champion's boxing boots, the turf still adhering to their scratched spikes.

The letter Dowling produced roused Gideon's immediate enthusiasm. Addressed from the office of *Wilkes's Spirit of the Times*, New York, and signed by the editor, George Wilkes, it relayed Heenan's interest in meeting Sayers, inquiring on what terms he might be placed on the challenge list. The attractions of a fixture between the Old and New World champions were obvious. For Dowling it augured unprecedented news value; for Gideon, the prospect of punters rich in dollar currency, and the chance to see his fighter king of two hemispheres. George Wilkes, enjoying much the same position in American boxing circles as Dowling held in Britain, was not a correspondent to be dismissed. Subject to Sayers's endorsement, Gideon agreed, he should be informed that an appropriate deposit would secure Heenan a title fight. Gideon undertook to contact Sayers without delay.

Since his conquest of Paddock, the Camden pugilist had taken life easily, 'starring it about the country', as one report had it, 'exhibiting himself and his trophies to hosts of admiring fans. He took a benefit here, a benefit there, a couple of benefits in one week somewhere else, and was everywhere well received.' It had been flattering and lucrative, if not the best way to keep in fighting fettle. He greeted success with droll enjoyment. Asked on one occasion to demonstrate his athletic prowess at a dinner to which he was invited, he had leaned back, lit a large cigar and surveyed the sporting toffs around him. When he was ready, he had answered dryly, he would be pleased 'to pass among the gentlemen and punch their heads'.

Gideon's concern was not merely to gain his assent to the proposed match, but to impress on him the dangers of complacency. With these intentions, Dowling's confidant departed London forthwith, heading for Tunbridge Wells, the fashionable spa in Kent renowned for its chalybeate waters. Here, Sayers had pitched camp, ostensibly to get into shape again. Gideon watched him as he exercised. Sayers looked, as indeed he was, a hard man. His lugubrious, rough-hewn face was stained brown by the same powerful astringent used to toughen his hands: a process known as 'pickling'. His bull-neck widened to shoulders of remarkable muscular development, the source of his lethal punch. The chest, clean of hair, was built firmly on a high waist, sturdy loins and lean thighs. But Gideon noted unpropitious signs. The breathing—slightly forced—the telltale thickness of the midriff, proclaimed a less than spartan regimen. Sayers was still indulging newly found appetites.

The syndrome was not rare. For the first time in a harsh life, the fighting bricklayer had cash to spare, and admiration. He had learned to forget, for a while at least, Camden and its problems. Gideon, who had seen many a bruiser succumb more quickly to good fortune than to the rigours of the prize-ring, was apprehensive. 'The prospect of a barney with the Yank did not abash Tom. He was of the opinion that foreigners were men of straw.' There was reason, Gideon responded, for doubting this. Charles Lynch, an American, had recently fought in England against a Welshman of repute named Dan Thomas. Lynch had lost, but his ability and pluck had raised comment. Sayers was unconvinced. He listened to Gideon, but the latter knew him better than to take his attention for concurrence.

Throughout their association, Sayers had doggedly pursued his own path. 'There was a sort of sublime indifference and quiet stoicism about him,' wrote a contemporary. 'He believed thoroughly in Captain Barclay [*a legendary trainer*], very slightly in magistrates, and not at all in most other repositories of advice.' Gideon returned to London assured that Sayers would accommodate Heenan; less certain that he viewed the prospect with due gravity. Sayers himself moved from Tunbridge Wells to Rottingdean, on the coast near the Brighton of his childhood. As a ragged boy, he had watched the smartly clad huntsmen of the Brighton harriers passing near Rottingdean. Now, against all professional wisdom, he joined them, charging across the Sussex countryside on horseback. A good rider might easily break a bone hunting. Tom Sayers liked horses—his earliest extravagances were a dun cob to drive, and a pony for his daughter—but he never learned to stay astride them. According to one of several Sussex anecdotes, a wagoner carting wood in the neighbourhood was surprised to meet the champion, unseated and muddy, trudging alone toward Rottingdean.

'Ye'll do y'sen more mischief atop yon beasts than in the ring, maister,' the driver warned. 'Climb aboard.'

Sayers's friends could only hope the interlude would pass before it cost him the championship. It did pass, but not before 'a severe shock to Tom's esteem made him put on his thinking cap'. In April 1859, under a sky as heavy with thunder as with moral admonition, the wayward bruiser kept a long-standing fixture few enthusiasts took very seriously. Bill Bainge of Gloucester, so ignominiously dismissed by Sayers two years earlier, had implored his sponsors for a chance to do better, especially to refute the imputations of his former second, Massey, who had called him 'a yellow cur'. According to Bainge, he had been poorly advised and ill at the time of the contest. When his backers, unimpressed, declined to re-invest in him, his father, a farmer, reluctantly raised the stake. The Fancy took the fight as no more than a formality. So great were the odds in favour of the champion that few punters thought the outlay worth making.

But Gideon was not happy. Sayers showed no sign of having trained seriously. Indeed, the ominous thickening of his waist was more pronounced than it had seemed to Gideon at Tunbridge Wells. Bainge looked in good shape. Whatever else happened, he asserted, he would make Massey retract his words. A mass of black cloud, tinged with purple, rolled overhead as, to the dismay of Sayers's corner, the champion began to puff and labour under the desperation of his foe's attacks. Manifestly suffering for lack of preparation, Sayers dropped in the seventh and was lucky to get up. Having done so, he went for a knock-out while his wind held.

In the end, his skill proved too great for Bainge. By the tenth, the Gloucestershire fighter was practically senseless, and advice that he concede came from all sides. He shook his head. 'I'm no cur,' he muttered, 'I'll show Massey!' He was nailed again. At this, his seconds began to haul him from the ring. Breaking free, he flung back at the champion, who floored him for the fourth time. Even as Sayers offered to shake hands, Bainge attempted to renew the fight. The clouds broke. Rain fell in torrents. It scattered the Fancy, but it did not wash the memory of the seventh round from Sayers's mind. The truth of the moment stayed with him.

Convincing as was the outcome, the press and many punters complained of the champion's lapse. One popular gamble, since takers had been scarce on a straight verdict, had been on Sayers winning in fifteen minutes. That he took, in fact, twenty-two, disgruntled his backers. Journalists spoke of his duty to gambling men. Wrote Dowling in sober vein: 'We feel we are only doing him a favour in impressing upon him the necessity in future of leaving no stone unturned to retain the confidence placed in him.' Dowling had in mind the transatlantic challenge. His words were barely off the press before a second letter arrived from New York which threw doubt on the issue. Seemingly, rival factions were bearing on George Wilkes, for the new missive, dated 29 March from his office, proposed a surprising alternative to his first overture.

DEAR SIR

Enclosed please find a draft for £200 sterling drawn in your favour on the Bank of Liverpool, which I have been requested to forward to you on behalf of Aaron Jones by his backers in order that you may deposit for him the necessary sum for a meeting with the Champion of England in six months. . . . The language with which Jones accompanies this draft is as follows: 'I, Aaron Jones, hereby challenge the winner of the coming fight [*Bainge v. Sayers*] to meet me in six months from that time for two hundred pounds and the Champion's belt. The fight to take place near London, and to be governed by the rules of the London Prize Ring.' Jones also requests me to say to you for him that he hopes Sayers will, for old times' sake, give him the first chance; but this is a consideration I have no right to press, having previously consented to lay before you the claims of John C. Heenan. Your sense of propriety will find a law for the matter and, I hope, likewise permit me to remain, yours very truly at command,

GEO. WILKES

No sooner had Dowling digested the change of news than a third letter arrived enclosing a deposit from Heenan's backers. Both Heenan and Jones were ready, it appeared, to advance the stakes to five hundred pounds a side, should Sayers wish it, to obtain the fight. Sayers's wishes were not readily ascertainable. At Claremont Square, he was seldom at home when the press called. His sister, Mary, recited a set piece: 'Tom's out on a run, sir. Might have gone anywhere. He's done a lot of running since the barney with Mr Bainge.'

8 Love Story

All punished and penitent,
Down on the knee,
I now bend to Adah
To avert an adieu.
Oh, let not thine eyes, love,
Look black upon me
Because mine are forced to
Look black upon you.
CINCINNATI HERALD
(with cartoon of Heenan on
his knees before Menken)

Adah Menken's desire to keep her wedding with Heenan out of the public eye—oddly uncharacteristic, he recognized later—encouraged idle rumour. The supposed immunity of the hardened stage trouper to love in its simple and devout form led cynics to suspect the worst of her. Heenan's friends saw a calculating hussy exploiting his trusting generosity. Some doubted they were actually married. To others, intimacy on any terms with a prize-fighter consigned Menken to the ranks of the notorious. Complained Frank Queen of the gossips: 'The association of Menken's name with that of Heenan has made her the target for almost every scribbler in the country, who has severally married her to Tom Thumb, James Buchanan [*the U.S. president*] and the King of the Cannibal Islands.'

The truth, according to an admirer, was that despite her designing approach to men, Menken had 'fallen head over heels in love with Heenan. Blood heated by southern suns overwhelmed with sudden passion the clear logic of her brain.' The 'Boy' appears to have been equally overcome. Pictures of them in the summer of 1859 conveyed their felicity. Heenan, then sporting a trim moustache, towered over a beaming Menken, who seemed, on his arm, no larger than a school-girl. Ribbon butterflies fluttered on the lace which adorned her breasts, and on the front of the skirt which billowed from a supple waist. A great white feather swept wing-like from her black hair. Heenan smiled broadly, flashily immaculate down to the kid gloves and swagger-cane. Passers-by on Broadway paused to watch them prome-nade.

The rhapsody was short-lived. It was unfortunate, perhaps, that the couple could not have met later. In years to come, when Menken's pretensions had been reduced to erotic spectacle and sentimental verse, the consolations of unsophisticated lovers meant more to her. Where the physical limitations of such admirers as Swinburne and the aged Dumas frustrated her, the attentions of rough and ready courtiers, often bruisers, brought Menken some contentment. Belatedly, she then looked back on Heenan as her true love. For the present, her ambition predisposed to disharmony. The amiable pugilist lacked the wit to cope with her aspirations and temperament. More his mark were the unexacting dolls of East Fourteenth Street.

Dismissing Heenan's public following, Menken left him in no doubt that the future belonged to her. Its pursuit was largely on ground he found alien. In Frank Queen, and more so Edwin James, they had mutual friends, but Menken increasingly turned to rarer characters. At Pfaff's, the bohemian *rendezvous* on Broadway, she cultivated not only journalists but such celebrities as Fitz-James O'Brien and Walt Whitman. Amid the poets and philosophers, the declamation and *delicatessen*, of Pfaff's cellar, Heenan was wholly lost. The affected sorrows and plaints of the *literati* bored him. Menken, devouring their moods, asserted his boorish insensitivity.

On the other hand, she made little attempt to like his own friends. Cusick, whose nervy restlessness angered her—'he paced up and down as if he would never stop'—regarded Menken with ill-concealed enmity. Hick trainer he might be, but Cusick knew a rout from a contest, and feared for his fighter. Gusting abuse and endear-ments with equal force, Menken bemused the 'Boy' with her passions and protracted sulks. 'To the end of her days,' according to one report, 'emotional crises, swift and unexpected in their incidence, intermingled with ominous calms in her conduct.'

Heenan himself was less than a model spouse. Accustomed to the easy ways of the sporting crowd, he gambled, drank and enjoyed the casual admiration of saloon girls. Regarding such habits as acceptable, he was unprepared for Menken's abrupt response. Few, by all accounts, can have witnessed such female rage. 'When her temper was aroused, Menken would throw a cataleptic fit that was terrible to witness.' The actress could be murderous, once attacking with a dagger a stage-manager who annoyed her. Heenan's only answer to her storms was confused retreat. Increasingly, he sought refuge at the sporting parlours, where the company was tough, rowdy and relatively innocuous.

*

It was at the 'Exchange', Houston Street, a saloon run by a fight enthusiast named Harry Hill, that Heenan first heard of the challenge by Aaron Jones. The news was serious, for if Sayers gave preference to his compatriot, Heenan's bid for the British title would be set back by many months. Cusick had cause to prowl with mounting nervousness. His fighter was drinking too much. The 'Boy' was losing condition and equanimity. In Cusick's view, an early departure for England, where Heenan would be away from Menken, was imperative. George Wilkes was not encouraging. Having transmitted the rival claims to Dowling, it was not his duty, he held, to vote priorities. In the background was the bearded figure of Morrissey. Many believed him a backer of Aaron Jones.

If so, he had modified his strategy by autumn, for Jones's backing inexplicably disappeared, leaving the 'professor' hard-pressed for cash. Morrissey had other plans for his money. Heenan's domestic problems were not lost on him. Journalists had made fun of the 'Benicia Boy's' predicament; the Fancy remarked his shaken confidence. In the eyes of his enemies, he was ripe for the taking, and they saw no better executioner than Sayers. Not only was Morrissey prepared to lay money on the Englishman—he was ready to advise Sayers personally on Heenan's ring-craft. When Jones at last deferred to the pressures of finance, John Morrissey looked forward to a spot of business in the Old World. Since Long Point, it had been unfinished business.

On 7 October, George Wilkes wrote to Dowling at *Bell's Life*:

MY DEAR SIR

I take pleasure informing you that Aaron Jones, conceding to the common desire on this side of the Atlantic to see Heenan have the first chance at Sayers for the Championship, has desired me to make forfeit the deposit staked for him. . . . I am very solicitous about this as, for special reasons, I want Heenan upon record as early as possible. I send this with a note to Sayers in which I apprise him of Jones's forfeit. Please preserve the note of Jones to me, and believe me to be yours ever truly at command,

GEO. WILKES.

In November, a representative of Heenan's backers, Frederick Falkland, a New York solicitor, left for London to settle the final terms. At the request of Heenan's camp, the stakes were fixed at the minimum requirement of two hundred pounds, Falkland explaining that, since Sayers was the favourite, his clients preferred to lay their surplus funds in the betting market. Sayers and his advisers being agreeable, articles were duly sealed and Heenan notified to sail as soon as possible. It could not be too soon for Jim Cusick. Relations between his fighter and Menken had reached explosion point. Informed that he intended to depart for England and go into training there, 'a dozen fiends, imprisoned in her nature, broke loose'. According to James, she flew at Heenan, eyes blazing, her fists clenched. Heenan struck her, then withdrew to the 'Exchange' to regret the blow.

On the last day of December, 1859, the challenger and Cusick sailed on the *Asia*, Menken notably absent from the fans assembled at the waterside. She did not sulk for very long. Seeking consolation among her press friends, she was introduced to Robert H. Newell, drama editor of the *Sunday Mercury*. Newell, to make a name in the Civil War as a satirist (he wrote as 'Orpheus C. Kerr'—office seeker), was influential in print but an unprepossessing man. The southern beauty who filled his drab Fulton Street office with seduction shattered his private life. Three years later, Menken rewarded Newell's devotion by marrying and discarding him within a few weeks. He remained disconsolate until his death. Meanwhile, as Heenan prepared for the big fight, Menken exploited the drama critic's contacts.

So far, she had declined to be billed as Mrs Heenan. Now, the stir of fight-fever made her think again. By adopting the more familiar name in her profession, she might capitalize on sporting interest. With Newell's help, Menken convinced the Bowery Theatre of the prospects. The result exceeded expectations. Drawn by huge placards proclaiming Mrs John C. Heenan, inquisitive New Yorkers packed the theatre for the opening night. 'Booming herself as Mrs Heenan was the first sensational move in her stage career,' declared Edwin James. More, it was the first demonstration of mounting public obsession with Heenan's fate.

9 A Rail Excursion

Thro' the silent hours of night,
Close beside a leafy thicket:
On his nose there was a Cricket,
In his hat a Railway-Ticket ...
EDWARD LEAR

In the late summer of 1859, while the fourpenny *Times* and such respectable penny papers as the *Daily News* and *Telegraph* discussed British operations in China and Garibaldi's successes, less respectable weeklies—*Lloyd's*, *Reynolds*, the *Dispatch* and others—carried gossip of what was to be the penultimate battle of Tom Sayers. Already, the champion had declared his intention to retire in 1860, after the American challenge. Assuming victory in that event, he would claim possession of the belt by virtue of having defended his title successfully for three years. Meanwhile, an engagement had been arranged which, though not involving the title, was of interest on two counts: 1, as a last chance to observe Sayers before the international; and 2, because, for the first time as champion, he was matched with an opponent of his own weight. After a succession of heavyweight victims, the notion was a novelty. Those who recalled Sayers's massacre of the middleweights wondered at the temerity of his adversary.

Bob Brettle of Birmingham, a glass-blower by trade, was no novice. Six years younger than the hard man of Camden, he held the scalps of several notable pugs, among them Jack Jones, a Portsmouth veteran, Job Cobley, known as the 'Enthusiastic Potboy', a black fighter named Bob Travers and Jem Mace of Norwich. The defeat of Mace in three minutes on Brettle's last outing was the most remarkable of his victories. Mace was a swarthily handsome ruffian, popularly thought to be of gipsy blood. In fact, though he had played the fiddle for a livelihood, his ancestry was firmly rooted in farm tenancy. Mace had succumbed to Brettle in the first round. Talk that he had thrown the fight gained some credence from the ease with which he subsequently trounced an experienced bruiser known as Posh Price.

But if Brettle's *coup* was questioned, his backers believed in it. Hailing the verdict as evidence of his class, they encouraged a fixture with Sayers. Ostensibly, Brettle's pretensions were supported by a gloved demonstration in which he had performed confidently against the champion. This was misleading. Like many maulers, Sayers was embarrassed by the horse-hair mufflers used for sparring, and seldom excelled in them. Brettle had yet to face the naked fists renowned throughout the Fancy.

The conditions were ratified at Sharp Swift's house. Since the belt was not at issue, Sayers offered two-thirds of the purse, staking four hundred pounds against two hundred. The open market gave him a safer margin, opening at 5 to 2 and quickly lengthening to 3 to 1. A few investors took 4 to 1 on Sayers. In the boozy surroundings of the Horseshoe, a stone's throw from the toppers and trulls of the Haymarket, one punter went so far as to propose two hundred pounds against twenty that Brettle would be licked in ten minutes. Cut by the insult, Brettle took the bet himself.

In Birmingham, the tale was different. Many of Brettle's adopted neighbours (he had been born at Portobello, near Edinburgh) considered him the most likely fighter since Bendigo to restore the prestige of the Midlands. He had something of Bendigo's cunning and agility. The Sayers camp was at pains to deny him the support of a Midlands mob. Gideon was determined that the contest should be held south of London, a journey beyond the pockets of Birmingham's roughnecks. For some time, he had explored the advantages of rail charter. Of the companies operating out of London, the South Eastern Railway was particularly accommodating to fight crowds. So much so, indeed, that the county authorities had complained to the Home Office.

According to recent magisterial strictures, the South Eastern Railway repeatedly offered excursion facilities 'to large bodies of persons whose avowed intentions were to commit a breach of the public peace'. It was a matter of embarrassment to the company's directors, for the board, headed by the honourable James Byng, included at least one justice of the peace. At the same time, cut-throat competition in the rail business was a strong inducement to accept the substantial profits to be had from fight excursions. Delicately, the board left the problem to its secretary, Samuel Smiles. Smiles, who had recently written a best-selling book entitled *Self Help*, a panegyric of great men with the moral 'Do thou likewise', was a tactful man. Earnestly assuring the authorities that fight excursions were not condoned by the company, he quietly undertook their expedition.

Mention of Smiles's arrangements was omitted from the company minutes. Dates and times of excursions were withheld until a late hour, and then released only on the grapevine of the sporting pubs. Train drivers were issued with sealed orders of destination, and other staff sworn to secrecy. The procedure did not vary much. Normally, the excursionists were disgorged at a quiet rural station an hour or two from London, the train stood by while the fight took place, then the crowd re-embarked before the county police could appear in force. The exercise was lucrative. Monster trains, assembled from old rolling stock—the Fancy expected little comfort—could be packed to capacity. Booking arrangements were left to the promoters, who sold inclusive tickets in the pubs and split the proceeds with the railway company. Often, several thousand pounds were involved.

A few months before the Sayers–Brettle contest, a South Eastern Railway fight excursion to Headcorn, Kent, had provoked a strenuous protest from the chief constable of the county. Smiles had responded that the arrangements lacked his authority, and there would be no repeat of the episode. Now, in conjunction with Gideon, he planned a larger excursion to Ashford, a short distance beyond Headcorn, where Gideon had found a battlefield. The departure was set for 7 a.m., 20 September, at London Bridge. The train, comprising thirty-six carriages, was jam-packed, two locomotives being needed to provide the power. By the time late arrivals were aboard, many the worse for a night on the capital, it was nearly eight o'clock.

Two hours afterwards, the market town of Ashford appeared through the engine smoke. Erupting from the mammoth train, the fight crowd took Ashford like an assaulting army. Joseph Conrad, writing later in the shadow of the grey church, could hardly have conveyed a more exotic scene. To the Ashfordians, the London Fancy was a foreign race. Surging after the ring 'commissaries', it burst through hedges and gardens, finally swarming the appointed field. Prominent among its personalities were the ring-maker, an old pug named Tom Oliver, and the veteran cockney caterer Dan Pinkstone, who served alfresco breakfasts on the moist turf. With the ropes up, the crowd marshals began to assert themselves, clearing the ringside and warning off known thieves. Billy Duncan, the pro in charge of the 'keepers', possessed an arm few 'gonophs' cared to argue with.

At eleven o'clock, Brettle's appearance was signalled by a cap hurled over the waiting crowd. Flanked by his seconds, he seemed relieved to receive a friendly welcome from the London fans. Producing a fifty-pound note, he immediately called for a taker at 3 to 1 against himself. He was about an inch taller than Sayers, rounder on the shoulders, with a fair complexion and artful eyes. Nobody took the bet. When his boots were examined, it was found that the spikes were unacceptably long and sharp. His seconds filed them, but Sayers, on arriving, cut the work short. He could, he boasted, 'give the geezer that much'.

Sayers was in good condition. His brown-stained countenance looked considerably older than Brettle's, but gave a granite-like impression. Gideon appeared confident. So did Harry Brunton, a jovial fight-trainer and Sayers fan. Many regular supporters of the champion were present. The lean pedestrian (racing-walker) Bob Fuller, a friend of Sayers, was a regular member of the entourage. So was Jimmy Holden, a former companion of David Morgan, the 'Fighting Dwarf', and himself a diminutive three feet six inches. Holden could recall the famous 'battle of the dwarfs', in which Morgan defeated McBean the 'Sawney' in thirty-seven minutes, fighting in a twenty-foot ring for stakes of five pounds. There was also an anonymous eccentric known to the Fancy as the 'Birdman'. Invariably clad in a cape, he appears to have regarded fight excursions as ornithological outings, exclaiming excitedly when fowl or field-bird passed overhead.

Sayers conducted the opening rounds of the ensuing combat with a disregard for urgency which might have been a deliberate slight on the supporter who had backed him to win in ten minutes. For three rounds, he stood lazily near the scratch, content to counter-punch, while Brettle circled crabwise, sniping warily. To Henry Miles, who favoured blood and thunder, the Birmingham fighter appeared 'shifty', resorting to a 'cunning peripatetic dodge ... queer manœuvring ... walking round and showing his muscle'. A more perceptive observer conceded his prudence. Though Sayers looked lethargic, his blows left unpleasant marks. Of the two men, he was both hit the more frequently and remained the less scathed.

The passing of ten minutes assured Brettle at least the proceeds of one bet before the pace of the fight changed. Dancing close to his adversary in the fourth round, he inflicted a deep wound on the leg with his steel spikes. The champion was still disconcerted by the injury when a lucky punch put him down. He came back in a sterner mood. Brushing aside a flurry from Brettle, he smashed a fist to the Midlander's forehead, then spun him off his feet with a shot to the left shoulder. Offers of 5 to 1 on Sayers were now refused. Brettle hung back, but Sayers walked in again. There was a sharp exchange at close quarters, and Brettle slumped to his hands and knees.

He came up for the last round in bad shape. His forehead had risen in a lump that took in his right eye. His nose was haemorrhaged; his lips were swollen and seeping blood. The blow on the shoulder had weakened his left arm. For a moment, he skirted Sayers, hitting tamely out of range, then retreating as the champion came at him. Trapped by the ropes, Brettle unleashed a last despairing right, missed, and took a second blow on the damaged shoulder. He went down in his corner, contorted with agony. Discovery of a dislocated arm closed the contest. Sayers had won in fifteen minutes. The London Fancy was jubilant. In Brettle, its favourite had disposed of the only credible competition left in Britain. Nobody America could produce was imagined capable of living with the champion.

It was well for the people of Ashford that the bulk of the excursionists were satisfied. A few eggs and hens disappeared with the receding crowd; some fruit from the orchards and gardens. Many locals took refuge behind bolted doors. But the rabble, if noisy, was good-natured, content on the whole with looting the hedgerows. Blackberries were in season. It might easily have been otherwise. An angry fight crowd could make havoc in a small town. As it was, the Fancy was gone by noon, packed back on the train, leaving a handful of euphoric drunks stranded in Kentish pubs.

Gideon and the South Eastern Railway could applaud themselves. Within the span of half a day, fighters, officials and spectators had been shifted sixty miles and back without mishap. The county police had been caught napping. The profits were considerable. Everything pointed to the merits of planning the forthcoming international by rail transport. It would, Smiles learned, be an operation of unprecedented magnitude, involving the need for more than one train, and the most vigorous secrecy. Magistrates throughout the home counties would be alert. But if it proceeded successfully, the takings would exceed any in rail excursion history. The South Eastern, Smiles told Gideon, would be more than interested.

II THE CRUSHERS

But how the beaks in wrath proclaimed amid the motley race,
That no prize-fight or milling match should then and there take place.
                                                    Victorian rhyme

10 The Yank in England

> *Bold banner-bearer from a foreign land,*
> *The one fair bark of hope from distant strand!*
> *Ha! Prythee have a care, Sir Thomas Sayers;*
> *Nor make cock-sure, ye backers and ye layers;*
> *For there is that about this Yankee wight*
> *Will shiver lances with our English knight.*
> 'captain alfred de kantzow,
> Twenty-Second Regiment'

The *Asia* docked at Liverpool from New York on 16 January 1860, a murky day concealing the sights of the port from its visitors. Great buildings, spectral in the grey fog, hinted at a land of unrivalled wealth and enterprise. For all the poverty defacing her society, Britain was far the world's richest country, considered—as America was to be sixty years ahead—the nation with the best and biggest of most things. Uniquely in Britain, urban dwellers outnumbered the rural population, her teeming cities the wonder of foreigners. Heenan and Cusick approached London with fascination. If Liverpool and the Midlands conurbations were impressive, the capital was awesome, the largest city in western civilization. More than twice as populous as New York, its sheer scale intimidated many new to it.

Not only the size of London, but the starkness of its contrasts enthralled strangers. Wreathed in its mists and eerily smoky lights, squalor and magnificence rubbed shoulders on every side. Here was 'at once the emporium of crime and the palladium of Christianity'; a home for millions and a Mecca of bleak loneliness. Heenan left no report of his impressions, but a compatriot, Henry James, noted his arrival in Victorian London thus: 'Dusky, tortuous miles in a greasy four-wheeler . . . immensity was the great fact . . . the miles of housetops and viaducts, the compilations of junctions and signals ... the low black houses as inanimate as so many rows of coal scuttles, save where at frequent corners, from a gin shop, there was a flare of light more brutal still than the darkness.'

Falkland had arranged an interval of some three months for training before the fight. He did not advise that much of it should be spent in London. Apart from its myriad temptations of the flesh, and its watchful detectives—the ubiquitous 'jacks' of the city force—the attentions of the London Fancy were likely to hinder work. Cusick, observing the plush and crystal splendours of such pleasure palaces as Westons, the Canterbury and the Oxford, with their racy entertainers and promenading 'pick-ups', agreed that Babylon was no place for an impressionable fighter. By early February, Heenan had vanished from London, smuggled south-west to the rolling Wiltshire countryside.

Secrecy was short-lived. On 16 February, *The Times* announced that the American was training at East Harnham, a village near Salisbury. The *Field* sent a man to locate the camp. Negotiating 'a high wall of flint and clay', he found himself on the overgrown lawn of what had once been a monastery farmhouse. Stone seats flanked a heavy door within an ancient porch. The occupants received the intruder hospitably.

'The door was thrown open by a well-educated and well-spoken New Yorker. The party consisted of three: this gentleman, the Benicia Boy and his trainer, a small man of restless energy. They had found the place by accident, they said, and chose it for its lonesomeness.' Heenan declared England a splendid country, but wondered if it ever had good weather. Pointing to a view of the downs on which he exercised, he led the visitor to a barn. 'You've seen the playground, now I'll show you the school,' he said. Rusting agricultural implements had been pushed aside, and the space filled with weights, pulleys, a punch-bag and dumb-bells. Later, the journalist was invited to share dinner at the training camp. 'A grass-fed ox provided the main course.'

Comparing Heenan's good looks and relaxed charm with the image of the average British bruiser, the reporter appears to have mistaken him for a sporting amateur. The 'Boy' talked of his life, but omitted his strong-arm stint for Tammany. His parents, Timothy and Mary Heenan, had lived in West Troy, New York State, where he was apprenticed from school, he recalled, as a machinist. Like Morrissey, he had succumbed to the lure of Californian gold, travelling west in 1852. He was then seventeen; a strong youth, soon made stronger by prospecting and foundry work. He had fought battles with the rough-necks who swarmed to the region, but these encounters were not in the regular prize-ring. In 1857, by when the Vigilantes had warned off many fighting men, Heenan had moved to New York, meeting Morrissey at Long Point in '58. By British standards, his pugilistic record was minimal, but his physique and athleticism stood out.

'His feats as a pedestrian during his work were extraordinary. Six miles and a bittock did he generally turn in plain walking, and many a spin and tie up did he give to some of our toe-and-heel walkers. His spins at the top of his speed, too, were not a little astonishing . . . he could on a pinch do his quarter in fifty-six seconds—not bad for a 14-stone man standing nearly 6 feet 2 inches.' The man from the *Field* left camp as full of praise as of prime beef. 'This aspirant to fistic honours is no illiterate visitor. If I may venture an opinion after noting his demeanour, I must yield to the notion that if he be not too well-bred for the work he has set himself, he will achieve it.'

The *Field* report, quoted in sections of the daily press, performed no service for Heenan's camp. If Salisbury had so far overlooked its New York visitors, such publicity ensured that the authorities must now act. Training at Harnham ceased to be feasible. None was more indignant than Britain's boxing journalists, the small band of specialists whose code forbade the disclosure of training sites. Stung by the *Field*'s scoop, *Sporting Life* reminded its readers of the 'extreme difficulty' of both keeping faith with the public and protecting the interests of the fighters.

'To assert that we are not in possession of facts of the most interesting nature would be untrue; yet how can we, consistently with our position, lay that before the public which could only endanger the safety of the men, but tend materially to the dreaded danger of proceedings on the part of the authorities? The greatest caution must be observed, and we dare not even hint at the contemplated steps of the backers now.'

Driven from Harnham, the Americans sought the guidance of a British expert on police evasion named Jack Macdonald. Macdonald, an experienced fight second and ring adviser, was a friend of Aaron Jones, who had mentioned him often in New York. He wore a walrus moustache which, in itself, was evocative of disguise, and seems to have placed his faith in mobility, for he shifted ground with disconcerting frequency. Leaving Wiltshire, the Americans found themselves within the space of a few weeks lodged in Somerset, Cambridgeshire, Northamptonshire, Leicestershire and Derbyshire. Cusick pleaded fretfully for a settled base. It was not easy, Macdonald responded, to hide 'a contraband package of more than six feet, with a pronounced Yankee accent, from thousands of diligent searchers'. But he thought that he knew the place—a house at Trent Lock, in Derbyshire, where Bendigo and Poulson had once trained.

Heenan's perambulations, closely followed by the English press, added fuel to the controversy surrounding the big fight. Most of the so-called 'quality' publications took a disapproving attitude. In a lengthy sermon touching on Spartan and Athenian *mores*, the introduction of German gymnasia in public schools, and the 'manly' literature of Walter Scott, the *Manchester Guardian* deplored the following of sport for gain.

> The circumstances attendant upon the proposed prize-fight between the champions of England and America have formed a text for general discussion upon the present position of muscular art in this country. Apart from the legal question, it is a point of considerable interest to determine whether morality demands that prize-fighting should be discountenanced. As the system is at present conducted, we believe it does. . . . Let us give free rein to the development of muscular art. Only let it be done with a pure and simple object. For here steps in the great objection to prize-fighting becoming a legalized institution of the country. The leading prize-fighters of the day, we are assured, are not the brutes they are generally represented to be. But they minister in a service which is injurious to others.
>
> The unhealthy excitement produced upon the thousands of frequenters of the prize-ring, chiefly consequent upon desperate betting among men who can ill-afford to lose, is the main evil which follows in the train of the prize-fight. The fighters themselves

perform their part for money; not to develop their manly energies; nor yet do they assist in developing the physical powers of those around them. Instead of going to witness a prize-fight, let men don the gloves and learn and practise the art of fighting for themselves. . . . Let us not turn pharisaically from what human nature demands, but rather seek to turn these impulses to effective service by rendering them a means of salutary recreation.

Others were less academic. The puritan lobby, powerful in local government, and not absent from Parliament—where the young Yorkshire M.P., Lord Lovaine, was particularly vociferous against prize-fighting—reacted strenuously, demanding legal action. Privately, magistrates might or might not sympathize with John Heenan; in the glare of publicity, the letter of the law could hardly be overlooked. The Derby authorities moved in. Five hundred yards from Heenan's new camp on the River Trent, the county boundary met those of Nottinghamshire and Leicestershire. No fighter who had trained there, boasted the landlord, one H. Rice, had failed to escape at will. Unfortunately for Heenan, his ability to spot an English 'jack' was less infallible than that of a native pug. Waiting until Macdonald was preoccupied, the Derby police surprised their man without difficulty.

The arrest of the American proved a sensation. Bound over by the Derby magistrates to keep the peace in the sum of a hundred pounds, he was besieged in the court building by an excited mob. When all efforts to clear the packed streets failed, a cab was ordered to the front door, a decoy leaving in Heenan's top-clothes to draw the rush. 'The cab was surrounded by an immense crowd, part enthusiastic, part incredulous, while Heenan, accompanied by one or two friends, walked quietly from the back of the building. Here, he was recognized, and another cab into which he speedily jumped drove off amid loud hurrahs. The two cabs, after driving around for a few miles, discharged their loads at the Royal Hotel, where Heenan and his friends dined. The Benicia Boy left Derby soon afterwards, returning to London before seeking fresh fields.'

Heenan remained uncomplaining, but Cusick was beside himself. Frantically, he told Falkland that the fight would have to be postponed while the 'Boy' made up lost training. Falkland consulted Dowling, through whose offices a deferment of the battle was at length arranged. The sporting press was critical. Had Heenan been wise, asserted *Sporting Life*, he would have been advised by boxing editors from the start.

Those who have had the management of his training have certainly bungled matters in the most abominable manner. Could anything be more absurd than to take up his training quarters in the first instance within a mile of a cathedral city, where saintly feelings and opposition were certain? There are plenty of obscure nooks in England, far removed from towns and cities, where he might have gone on training till doomsday without the slightest fear of hindrance. Not only was this want of judgement exhibited in the selection of quarters, but writers of the press were admitted to his presence to give him greater notoriety, and he may thank these 'friends' for being chivied all over the country.

Macdonald, in a letter to *Bell's Life*, denounced the critics as 'judges and juries comfortably in session behind their pipes and glasses'. Heenan laughed at the printed squall. For the 'Benicia Boy', popularity outweighed cavil and inconvenience. He had come to England ignorant of the country and its people, half in fear of public hostility. Being liked was important to the amiable American; the approbation of the Derby crowd, and others, a tonic to his morale. That he owed it to the opponents of prize-fighting was ironical. Wrote the *Liverpool Telegraph*:

There are two things which people must have—something to eat and something to talk about. Heenan is famous when Louis Napoleon ceases to interest: and the diligence of press correspondents has made scores of rural policemen jump in connection with the Yankee pugilist. It were a blessing if other pugnacious individuals were pursued with the same zeal, for then fighting sovereigns would be more disposed to keep the peace. Heenan cannot seek concealment in places most remote without finding a constable on his trail; while vigilant magistrates, in their abhorrence of peace breakers, cannot be aware that they are playing the game of the Fancy. They are increasing the interest in the fight for the championship, making the prize public, provoking more betting and hedging. Heenan is a hero. People want to know all about his history, his wife and his whereabouts. When the fight takes place, the crowd will be immense. The telegraph will be taxed to spread the result abroad, and sporting houses will be chockfull of gamblers, boxers and other disreputable characters. If the magistrates and police are trying to prevent this they are trying in the wrong way.

11 Fresh Air and Blue Pills

*Eleven stone of sinewed might
Has trained by day and dreamed by night
Of Ecstasy, the perfect fight,
Life's triumph, Beauty stark.*

ANON.

*You may as well try and dam the gut of Gibraltar
with a sluice made of wafers as go into the ring
without training.*

FISTIANA

One result of the hunting of Heenan was that Sayers was left alone. Early in February, he left London for Newmarket, on the borderlands of Suffolk and Cambridgeshire. With its many stables and gallops, its heath and chalk downs, the district was among the champion's favourite training haunts. Horse-racing and prize-fighting traditionally shared common ground. Pugilists performed at the fairs which accompanied race meetings; jockeys and stable lads frequented the ringside. To a large extent, the following of the two sports was identical, and their organizers took care that major fixtures—the classic races and championship battles—should not clash. At the racing town, Sayers was among friends. He was the toast of the pubs, and on the free list at the race track.

All the same, he left Camden reluctantly. His daughter was twelve; young Tom a boisterous nine-year-old. Parting from them for ten weeks or more was a hard wrench. His wife had now produced a second infant by her Pimlico paramour—a boy christened Alfred Aldridge to join James Aldridge in the nursery—and, though Sayers had again increased her allowance, it might be wondered if his own two children would suffer. While he lived with his sister, Mrs King, he saw them regularly, walking with them while Sarah rode her pony and young Tom romped with his father's dog, Lion. The animal, a tawny mastiff, had become the champion's mascot.

Sayers took his leave gloomily. Mary King had tidied the children for their return to their mother when Henry Miles turned up in search of copy. It was a bad moment to be asking questions, and Sayers was not pleased. Dispatching the youngsters with a last hug, he turned to his packed bag. Mrs King saw his fists clench. 'Fighting, guv'nor?' He forced a grin. 'Is that all you think about?'

Miles had a warm heart. Bluff in manner, he was kindly in deed. But he was tactless. Whether from misguided chivalry, single-minded devotion to boxing, or perhaps both, he seems not to have noticed that fighters had private lives. In all his voluminous writings on the fist sport, he virtually ignored the existence of women. As the biographer of Sayers, he excelled himself, producing a life of his hero, albeit a sketchy one, without a hint of the torment central to his subject. Of the fighter's wife, their home, Alfred Aldridge, Aldridge's children, the author might have been oblivious. None was mentioned.

Miles's readers now learned that Sayers had left 'gaily' for an undisclosed training base. There, 'without a care in the world but for Heenan's nob', the champion would prepare for 'the *coup de maître* of fistic history'. Had Sayers been able to read, he might have been impressed. As it was, though he trained conscientiously, he seems not to have taken special steps for the occasion. British patrons and managers regarded a two to three months' physical build-up as normal before their men fought. Dowling, whose manual encompassed the approved regime, advised 'all backers never to patronize, and all sporting men never to bet on the man who will not submit to a regular course of training'.

The objectives were to increase strength, wind and agility. It was also considered important to develop what the Fancy called 'bottom', the capacity to endure prolonged exertion and punishment. To this end, a strict embargo was placed on the indulgences habitual to many bruisers. 'Spirits, porter, gross feeding, stimulants, tobacco, onions, pepper and sexual intercourse must vanish,' insisted *The Oracle of the Ring*, 'and be no more heard of within the first week.' Isolation from female company was emphasized. 'Indulgence with women is every bit as bad as indulgence with wine. Indeed, the one leads to the other; both enfeeble, undermine, and at last prostrate the constitution.' Fighters in training were encouraged to wash in soapy water until 'the long-adhering dirt and grease can be got rid of'. At a time when cleanliness, in many quarters, was more preached than practised, Dowling admitted that a man might 'feel repugnance at washing the body'. Nevertheless, washing was imperative, followed by rubbing with coarse linen, and a brisk walk.

In the second week of training, sweating was encouraged to displace flesh. The effect was procured by hard exercise in flannel clothing, or, at night, by warm wraps and possets (drinks made of hot milk curdled with ale). On a fine day, exercise commenced with a trot before breakfast, extending gradually, for Sayers, from two miles to four miles. In the event of damp or windy weather, the *Oracle* recommended indoor activities: 'Spar at home, grind the meal, rub down a horse, play at ninepins, leapfrog, or any manly exercise.' After breakfast, came a walk punctuated by bursts at speed.

> While jogging along, the conversation should be of the pleasant sort; viz., concerning the coming battle, former encounters, how battles are won and lost, and so on. All at once, or by preconcert, a mile run at nearly top speed is to be knocked up. Next day, two, and soon after, three miles may be done. Then the propriety of being at home to meet the patron, or see some friend with whom to have an agreeable chat or play, will bring the trainer and the trained back to headquarters.

Fighters in training were sparred heavily once a day, as near as possible to the hour for which the actual fight was scheduled. 'The sham fight should resemble the forthcoming encounter. Combining the peculiar tactics of his man's opponent, his mannerism, language, accent and vulgarisms, the trainer in sparring must endeavour to imitate them all. The sparring should continue for an hour at shortest, including a bout or two after dinner is announced.' Boxers were advised to retire to bed early. 'Going to bed should be gone about pleasantly, and take place in an airy chamber with chimney, but without curtains of any sort, on a hard bed with coarse linen.' An open window was recommended, subject to individual susceptibilities. 'Much must depend on the former habits of the man. If he has been stove-bred in the populous purlieus of a large town, he may find the rare air of the country overpowerful. Be he country bred, a cottager or labourer, the trainer must not hesitate as to the free admission of fresh air.'

A good trainer—more particularly, an honest one—was held invaluable. Pugilism was organized by, and for, gambling men. Many speculated as much on the trustworthiness of trainers as on the fighters.

> The backer and his agents or friends must bring into play all their arts to discover this vital fact, this leading move on the board, around which all subsquent play will centre ... bets, stakes, laying-on and edging-off, all rest upon this main point of faithfulness in the trainer ... either he should be placed above a bribe, or be so closely watched in his movements as to render clear the detection of unfaithfulness.

Trainers were employed by backers or sponsors, to whom they reported progress much as race-horse trainers reported to owners. Dowling stressed the analogy: 'A man put to training is like a colt to be broken in.' Not only his body but his spirit needed schooling. 'Let the trainer talk of nothing but how the victory is to be obtained, and show his man how. Lead the soul along, and the body must follow. Yet guard him against blind confidence, and tell him of his faults.' Supervision varied in style with the status of the pugilist. As a champion of unique prestige, Sayers controlled his own regimen, assisted rather than directed by those hired to care for him. Diplomatically, Gideon and his colleagues placed the main responsibility on the champion's old admirer Harry Brunton, sometime pug and publican, whose cheerful personality buoyed the knotty pugilist. Also in attendance was a smart ring-second named Jemmy Welsh, a lean-faced stalwart with straggling whiskers and a ready wit.

Most good fighters had their foibles. Old Dutch Sam, a famous name of the past, would only train on gin. Sayers worked best around stables, relaxed in the company of dumb beasts. But, for the most part, principles were agreed. The consumption of spirits was not advised. Some trainers believed in denying their men beer, though in general its moderate use was thought wholesome. Dowling specified a pint a day of home-brewed, made of hops, malt and water (three bushels of hops to the barrel). London-brewed liquor was proscribed, as was the consumption of ale from more than one brewery on the same day, 'for the variety of proportions and kinds of ingredients will, if nought worse, derange the bowels'.

Wine was sometimes recommended for those who reduced too much. 'If such an one take his dinner of roast or boiled meats, using salt, and drink a glass of pure old port at two or three sups in the intervals of eating, he will make blood faster than any other means we know.' Hot tea and coffee were held unfit for pugilists. If they demanded such 'catlapperies', stated the *Oracle*, the beverage should be served lukewarm. Far preferred was the great Victorian cure-all of water-gruel, a thin dilution of salt and oatmeal—'the all-potent iron prince of health and strength'.

Dowling, at his most pedantic on the choice of food, instructed trainers to provide two substantial meals a day: breakfast at 8 a.m. and dinner at 2 p.m. or 5 p.m. Suppers, he maintained, were injurious to the lungs.

> The only meat that need be used in training is good beef and good mutton. All young meat such as veal and lamb, all white flesh, whether game or poultry, are good for nothing. They contain no nourishment for the muscle. Soups, fish, pies, puddings must be left to the club-house gourmands; they are poison to the boxer. His animal food should be rump-steaks (good ox-beef) and mutton (wether) chops, slightly broiled and with every particle of fat cut away. All oily messes, melted butter, buttered toast and gravies are to be eschewed. . . . Mustard, pepper and all hot spices are prohibited as producing a high stimulus and consequently reducing the volume of muscle by absorption.

Vegetables were disfavoured, with the exception of potatoes when dry and mealy. Bread had to be of the right kind. 'Trainers should avoid giving their men London-made bread, which is anything but the staff of life. Light country-made bread, well baked and two days old, is what the boxer is to eat with his meat, and the trainer should take care to have dry biscuit always at hand; a small bit taken as soon as the eyes open in the morning is an excellent absorbent of the accumulated mucus of mouth, throat and windpipe.'

Frequently, the morning biscuit came with a physic. The average trainer administered potions and medicines with the zeal of a fraudulent coper. Even Dowling, no slouch in the area of quackery, complained that 'medicines are generally relied upon too much'. Bleeding, purging and induced vomiting were common standbys. Boxers who were peevish during work-outs, grunted or groaned in their sleep, or 'showed sallow'—accepted symptoms of poor condition—could expect to be dosed. So could those whose skin had more colour in some parts than others. Excitability indicated that a pugilist was due for 'a brisk cathartic', after which he would be bled.

Dull heavy eyes, with a great disposition to sleep, or pricking of the skin, demand that a man should be blooded. Opening physic should always go with bleeding. . . . Vomiting may be used when the stomach is foul, and to get rid of crudities not cleared by purging. It must be resorted to when the pugilist feels nausea, has a hot fetid breath, or a tongue furred and white in the morning. If it is not done, subsequent food and exercise will be wasted. The pugilist will not gain in strength.

Fighters were induced to vomit by a mixture of tartar emetic and ipecacuanha (the root of a South American shrub) worked off by warm camomile tea. Most trainers used aloes and/or salts as purgatives. One regime, known as 'three threes', comprised three doses of salts, three sweats and three vomits for three weeks. Dowling, condemning this as too drastic, placed his faith in various brands of pills, the mass production of which was still a novelty. His favourite was 'the blue pill', taken with a mild infusion of senna. Manufactured at Apothecaries' Hall, the blue pill contained mercury. Dover's powders were a popular sudorific, or sweater. 'Ten grains will sweat a little one, twelve for a stronger man, and fifteen for a big one.'

Some methods, including the use of body or flesh brushes on

fighters, smacked of the stables. 'In training racehorses, indeed, friction is much better understood and more practised than in the training of men,' wrote Dowling. 'On the principles laid down we say that, if you rub the skin till it glows, you will stimulate the pores into healthy action and draw blood to the part rubbed. . . . We should advise the daily use of the flesh brush, for about a quarter of an hour morning and evening. Nothing acts more powerfully on the wind, and on the process of digestion.'

Brunton, like many trainers, used farriers' oils on stiff joints, and a veterinary compound called opodeldoc (soap, spirits of wine and camphor) on painful ligaments and tendons. Another embrocation was prepared by dissolving camphor in spirits and mixing the solution with almond or olive oil. No thoroughbred at Newmarket was better provided for than the prize-fight champion.

12 For the Record

Oh, it is life to see a proud
And dauntless man step, full of hopes,
Up to the P.R. stakes and ropes,
Throw in his hat, and, with a spring,
Get gallantly within the ring;
JOHN HAMILTON REYNOLDS

There are two things that an Englishman
understands, hard words and hard blows.
Nothing short of this (generally speaking)
excites his attention or interests him in
the least.
WILLIAM HAZLITT

The revival of interest in prize-fighting occasioned by Heenan's challenge surpassed the most sanguine forecasts of the patrons. Openly or covertly, people of all types scanned the press for information. Few journals were so smug as to disregard the approaching fight. Asserted the London *Times*: 'Much as decent people deplore the affair, there is no disguising the fact that this challenge has led to an amount of attention being bestowed upon the prize-ring which it has never received before.' It might have been added that much of the attention came, in fact, from 'decent people'. Shudder as they did at the antics of the Fancy, the middle classes of the period could scarcely ignore an issue involving the prestige of British manhood, of bulldog grit. Patriotism transcended even respectability.

Suddenly, undertakers and grocers, civil servants and drapers—solid citizens normally aloof from vulgar sports—clamoured to learn more about the common knuckle-fighter. Who was the English St George of boxing, and where had he come from? Questions about Sayers's career and origins appeared over and again in the 'Answers to Correspondents' sections found in most journals. Information was scrappy. Profile-writing was not a feature of Victorian sports journalism. The public depended for its knowledge of 'celebrities' on snippets of intelligence gleaned from writers generally more verbose than revelatory, or the editors of the 'Answers' columns—often inky juniors armed with well-thumbed encyclopaedias.

What they could not find out, they sometimes invented. According to the premier boxing medium, *Bell's Life*, the British champion's family 'came from Dingle, in the county of Kerry, Southern Ireland', where an ingenious pedigree attributed him with the blood of 'the battling Fitzgeralds'. Such information must have surprised the very English Sayers clan, whose flavour was as redolent of Sussex as Pulborough eels and coger cakes. The fighter's father, William—known as 'Old Tan' for his leathery complexion—was a cobbler.

William Sayers hailed from Storrington, near Steyning. He was baptized there, and there he had married Mary Pickard, a serving maid. Tom Sayers was their fifth child. By the time of his birth, the family had settled in Brighton, then the largest town in southern England outside London. Its growth in a few decades from an insignificant fishing village had come about largely due to the publicity attending a fashionable doctor named Richard Russell, who established a sea-bathing clinic there. Led by the Prince Regent, health-seeking London society had taken the road to Brighton with its bathing wraps. But the Brighton of the Regent's Pavilion and elegant Georgian houses was not that of cobbler William Sayers and his family. Their home was in a row of poor tenements, 'mean and fishy', leading from Church Street to North Lane.

From here, instead of attending school, young Tom was sent barefoot to the beach to earn pennies pushing fishing and pleasure boats from the shingle which banked the water's edge. One day, when he was eleven, Sayers assisted a couple named Machin to put out in a rowing boat. The Machins were later washed ashore, drowned. As a witness at the inquest, the boy was obliged to identify the corpses. It was the symbolic end of his childhood. By now, the profitability of the London–Brighton run had attracted the railwaymen, and the building of an impressive station and viaduct at the resort meant steady work for labourers and artisans. Sayers was apprenticed to the trade of bricklaying.

Few even of the regular Fancy knew much of the champion's introduction to fighting. In his early teens, it seemed, Sayers had taken to hanging around the Brighton 'academy' of Jack Phelps, the local boxing pro. Hod-humping had invested the stocky youth with precocious strength, and he fancied his chances in the roped square. At sixteen, he stood his first test. He had joined the spectators of a prize-fight near Brighton race-course when, the main bout over, a Sussex bruiser named Haines challenged all-comers for a small stake. Sayers produced his money. He was overmatched in age, weight and experience, but already carried a man's punch. Haines was hugging to escape an unexpected pounding when the appearance of a local magistrate cut the fight short.

Completion of the railway works at Brighton induced Sayers to move to northern London, where similar construction opportunities had opened. Among the metropolitan 'brickies', some rashly scornful of his Sussex accent, he quickly gained a fighting reputation. Then a pound short of ten stone, taciturn with grey, faintly puzzled eyes, he looked deceptively vulnerable. Only those who had seen him in action were undeceived. At that time, the fancied mauler of the district was Abe Crouch, twelve stone, a couple of good victories to his name. It was Crouch's boast that no man in North London dared meet him at his own weight, and he laughed when Sayers was mentioned. When the bricklayer's friends put ten pounds on the outcome, Crouch cheerfully matched the stake. The fight, at Greenhithe, on 19 March 1849, was Sayers's introduction to the regular prize-ring. He marked the occasion by nailing his man in twelve minutes.

Though the emergent Sayers had 'much to learn in the *tactique* of the boxing art', journalists did not doubt his toughness. Miles, for one, recalled the surprise of several veterans on witnessing 'the remarkable strength and resolution' of the novice. A year later, his performance against an intelligent middleweight, Dan Collins, proved Sayers an apt pupil in the finer points of the knuckle game. During eighty-four minutes at Long Reach, on the Thames, he comprehensively outboxed his maturer opponent. 'The great improvement of Sayers on this occasion was evident to every judge of boxing; he took a strong lead, was never headed, and won in a canter.' Still, he was fighting for 'small beer'. It was not until the summer of '52, according to the records, that he was staked for a hundred pounds.

His adversary that June was a redoubtable Southwarkian, Jack Grant, a man who had beaten James Haggerty and Alec Keene, top-class middleweights. He stripped about six pounds heavier than Sayers and was priced 7 to 4 favourite. The scrap, at Mildenhall, Suffolk, was notable as the first really prolonged ordeal Sayers experienced, an early indication of the generalship with which he would sweep the field of British middleweights. Sayers, advised between rounds by his loyal supporter Fuller, the long-distance walker, paced himself better, hit harder and, after more than two hours in the ring, out-lasted the Southwarkian. Commented *Bell's Life*:

> Tom Sayers by this victory has established a reputation as a man of science, courage and endurance. The manner in which he stopped the determined attacks of his adversary, the judgement with which he extricated himself from difficulty, refusing to struggle for the fall with a stronger man, proved that his head was screwed on the right way, and that, although a novice compared with his opponent, he was perfectly acquainted with the theory of his art. . . . He proved himself a very hard hitter, managing to get onto his opponent so frequently that Grant's iron mug displayed bumps and contusions it has seldom exhibited. Sayers is a good-tempered, well behaved young fellow with a high character of honour and integrity. We trust that success will not in his case, as in many we could name, destroy good principles.

More than one journal, previewing the Heenan title contest, recalled the Grant episode. But another battle of the past claimed greater press space. Almost every analysis of the champion's prospects against Heenan touched on a combat Sayers's supporters rarely mentioned: his single defeat in almost two decades. Were it possible for Sayers to lose to the American, such a tragedy, it was inferred, might in some way follow the pattern of that lone failure. Heenan himself was said to have contemplated the possibility. The question fell in two parts: 1. How had Sayers been beaten? 2. Could the 'Benicia Boy' profit from history?

Nathaniel Langham, the only man to have vanquished the champion, was an affable, dimple-chinned villager from Hinckley, Leicestershire. He had worked on a farm before buying a horse and van, with which he ran deliveries. At eleven stone, an unpopular weight between the middle and heavy men, he was often obliged to overmatch himself. By the time he met Sayers, Langham was thirty-three, eight years the senior, already known as 'Old Nat', or 'Clever Nat'. Among other things, he was a pastmaster at landing a straight left, his favourite shot, then slipping to the ground to escape retribution. Since deliberate falls were against the rules, the tactic demanded not only theatrical talent but, ideally, underfoot conditions which made slipping credible. The day before the fight, a Monday, rain fell ceaselessly. On Tuesday, an autumnal sun glanced on palpably greasy grass. Langham could not have wished a better morning.

The battle took place at Lakenheath, Suffolk, before a small and orderly gathering. By an oversight, the fixture had been set for the opening day of Warwick races, to which the bulk of the sporting roughs had diverted. As a consequence, profits were poor, but ring-control immaculate. An exceptional feature of the contest was the number of rounds, sixty, crowded into a duration of two hours. Allowing half a minute between rounds, the average bout was no more than ninety seconds, an indication of the constancy of Langham's tactics. From the outset, the Leicestershire man tumbled like a March hare. Reaching a long arm over Sayers's guard, Langham would leave his mark and drop before an answer was delivered. In the first twenty rounds, he was down every time, twice genuinely from punches, otherwise 'playing the saving game'.

In the twentieth, Langham took a full-blooded knock-down blow. Sayers followed it in the next round with a left and right to head and body, then threw his opponent with a back-fall. The betting, having opened on Langham, swung significantly the other way. Indeed, Langham looked weak in the twenty-third. For several rounds he went down at the slightest provocation until, regaining equilibrium, he began scoring again with straight punches. By the hour mark (twenty-ninth round) there seemed little between the men in fitness. Sayers, the stronger fighter, was boring in with combinations of punches to all parts of the target, generally winning the wrestling bouts. Langham exploited his longer reach with straight dabs, poking his left into Sayers's face. An ugly puffiness round Sayers's eyes increasingly attracted Nat Langham's fist.

Of the situation by the thirty-ninth round, a witness reported:

Although appearances were in favour of Sayers, there were many who saw the danger before him, and among these must assuredly be numbered Nat's seconds, by whose directions Langham now devoted himself to land on Tom's swollen eyes, then to get down with as little exertion as practicable; for it was impossible to conceal Nat's weakness, and a moot point whether he would be able to hold out until Tom could be forced to put up the shutters. Nat tried to lead off but was stopped. Sayers attempted to return, but Nat sent out his left very straight to the eye, and on Sayers again coming on, at once went to grass.

Langham appears to have played his game with great skill, for no protest was recorded at the falls which kept him in the fight. In the forty-fifth round, taking a Sayers left to the cheek, he went down visibly sickened. In the forty-sixth he did nothing but stay on his feet until a chance came to slide to earth. The 'breather' restored his strength. Next round, he placed a stinging shot on Sayers's right eye, following it in the forty-eighth with two jabs to the left eye. It was a crucial stage in the contest. For the first time, Sayers took the fall, and it was not an academic one. His eyes were so nearly closed that only by lancing the flesh around them were his seconds able to return him with any sight. He came up for the forty-ninth bleeding from both sockets, desperate to conclude the battle before his vision went.

Langham held on grimly, pushing out his left, tumbling more from weariness now than intentionally. 'Both were nearly pumped out, and it was evident that a chance hit might finish Langham, while Sayers, if he could not deliver it, must soon quit.' Sayers opened the sixtieth with a rush. Langham avoided him, jabbing to the eyes and mouth, then, as Sayers whirled, to the right ear. Both fell. 'Beyond a doubt, Sayers could not see what he was doing, and there were cries from his backers to pull him off, but Tom refused to give up.' Swinging his arms, he stumbled to scratch and lunged at Langham. The blows were off target. Langham waited his chance, then delivered two shots, one to each eye. Sayers shuddered and groped sightlessly for his corner. It was over.

Perhaps wisely, Nathaniel Langham avoided a return fight by announcing his retirement from the prize-ring. That he had confirmed his reputation for astuteness was certain, but whether Heenan had anything to learn from his victory was less so. By 1860, seven years had elapsed since the contest. Meanwhile, Sayers, growing in stature and experience, had beaten bigger and better adversaries. There was another consideration. On dispassionate evidence, Langham's achievement appears to have been somewhat diminished by the condition of Sayers before the fight. He had caught a bad cold during training, and may have had a virus infection on the day. Observers spoke of an ugly eruption on his face and neck, suggesting some disorder of the blood. It may have weakened his resilience to head injury, for harder hitters than Langham had failed conspicuously to make the same impression on Sayers's face.

For all of which, the champion himself found the lessons worth remembering. Much of his success in the ring against big men was due to his mastery of tactical falling, an art he might not have perfected but for Langham's example, while he never forgot his loss of vision. The possibility of saving the day by calculated blinding was stored in his mind for emergencies.

13 A Breath of Scandal

Some day, Ed., I am going to be the greatest
artiste in the world

ADAH ISAACS MENKEN

Poor impious Soul! that fixes its high hopes
In the dim distance, on a throne of clouds,
And from the morning's mist would make the ropes
To draw it up amid acclaim of crowds

ADAH ISAACS MENKEN

At Great Scotland Yard, Whitehall, the Commissioner of the Metropolitan Police Force, Sir Richard Mayne, discussed the fight issue with his officers. Mayne was a good policeman, and a pragmatist. The course agreed was strict adherence to standing policy: namely, by surveillance and an adequate show of strength, to drive the Fancy into the countryside for its sport. What happened in the shires was not Mayne's responsibility. At the suggestion of Superintendents Hannant and Durkin ('A' and 'F' divisions, respectively), it was resolved that detectives familiar with London's sporting haunts should make a point of listening for news of the venue. Particular attention would be given to the George and Dragon, Barbican, the house of Sayers's trainer, Harry Brunton, and to Southwark, a district with a fighting tradition. The Southwark manor was doubly significant, being contiguous to the southern railway and London Bridge terminus.

The Times claimed the first firm intelligence. On 24 January, under the leader 'Forthcoming Great Prize Fight', it confided on a modest note:

Without pretending any special knowledge about the great prize-fight of which all sporting men are talking, we may mention that it is to take place on the 16th April, and that it will be fought privately, though not perhaps confidentially, not very far from Mildenhall, a little village town in Suffolk, on the Eastern Counties line of railway. Mr Smiles, the secretary of the South Eastern Railway, was applied to, if our information be correct, for a special train along this line, but, as might have been expected, the concession has been refused. The shareholders will probably endorse this decision at their approaching half-yearly meeting in the event of the question being then raised.

Justifiably, for the report could hardly have proved more inaccurate, few counties within excursion range of London were reassured by its pronouncements. In Surrey, where the authorities, led by the magistrates and the Lord Lieutenant, the Earl of Lovelace, had long since declared war on prize-fight crowds, law officers were told to ignore the Suffolk story and be vigilant in their own neighbourhoods. Hertfordshire, also discounting *The Times* report, took its own steps. In Hertford, the Chief Constable, Colonel Archibald Robertson, made application to the justices for a warrant to apprehend Sayers and Heenan in order that they might be bound over to keep the peace.

Robertson was unequivocal. He possessed, he said, positive information that the fight was to take place in Hertfordshire, and that at least eight thousand spectators would accompany the pugilists. 'There was no knowing what mischief might be done by the irruption of thousands of persons of the class likely to assemble at a prize-fight.' The bench, under its chairman, Thomas Mills, M.P., promptly granted a warrant requiring the fighters to find substantial sureties. The justices, said Mills, were 'determined to prevent the contest taking place within their boundaries'. Other authorities echoed the sentiment. Colonel Robertson, it appeared, was not the only police chief with special intelligence.

As one county after another proclaimed itself endangered, the presumed journey between London and the venue stretched incredibly. Within days of the Hertford warrant, articles of peace against the pugilists were exhibited in Warwickshire, the chief constable 'having received information leading him to suppose beyond question that the combat will ensue there'. It must have seemed to the organizers of the battle, particularly to Gideon, who had undertaken to find a site, that their own indecision at that stage was singular.

*

In America, excitement spread with equal rapidity. As a newspaper topic, the forthcoming fight transcended interest even in the quotable Abraham Lincoln, whose nomination as Republican candidate for presidency was imminent. Popular emotion, rooted nostalgically in the past, bestowed on Heenan the spirit of George Washington. 'In those days,' wrote a chronicler of the period, 'a favourite entertainment with the New York public was the Revolutionary drama, in which one Yankee easily whipped half a dozen Britishers.' Sayers, after all, was only one Britisher. Not only in New York, but in most other cities of the republic, Heenan was seen as an emissary of American superiority, set to trounce John Bull on his own estate. Informed sportsmen, if more cautious, were still eager for the hour of truth. Scores of gamblers, journalists and fight-fans reserved passages for England.

The name 'Heenan' possessed a magnetic charm. After the success of her opening at the Bowery, Adah Menken continued to draw crowds as the fighter's wife. What she did, how she did it, was of little importance. She was willing to try her hand at most things. Within a few months, she appeared in repertory and variety, in a minstrel act, in support of Blondin the rope-walker, and in company with Sam Cowell, the comedian. She did imitations of Charlotte Cushman and Edwin Booth. She danced. She sang 'The Captain with his Whiskers gave a Sly Wink at Me'. If critical acclaim was negligible, no one expected virtuosity. While Heenan's remained a name to conjure, Menken could depend on public interest. It was as well she could, for she had no savings; the 'Boy' no income until the fight.

Apart from billing herself at the theatre as Heenan's wife, Menken appended his name to the verses Newell placed for her in the *Mercury*. These fetched a modest price. Derivative in style, shot with melancholy, they were hardly the stuff to rouse the Fancy. '*Yes, yes, dear love! I am dead! Dead to you! Dead to the world! Dead for ever! . . . How did I die? The man I loved—he—he—ah, well! There is no voice from the grave. The ship that went down at sea, with seven times a thousand souls for Death, sent back no answer.*' Menken's poetry was persistently funereal. But one reader, at least, got a jolt from it. Detecting echoes of Mrs John C. Heenan in the mid-west, Alexander Menken, son of the dry-goods merchant, identified her as his departed wife. It seemed to him strange she should be posing as the wife of the pugilist, for, as he told the Cincinnati press, her first marriage was not dissolved. She had left Alexander; he had never freed her.

The understanding of the parties is now obscure. Whether Adah Menken believed herself released from her first marriage or not is debatable. Conceivably, she had been promised a divorce by Alexander, and had mistaken the word for the action. Either way, she could not have become Heenan's legal wife, because only now did Alexander institute divorce proceedings. Curiously, since there was no subsequent wedding, Adah Menken sued Heenan for divorce at a later date. Stranger still, Judge Isaac G. Willson of the circuit court, McHenry County, Illinois, granted it—a rare case, it would seem, of the legal dissolution of a marriage which had never been legalized.

At all events, New York was left in no doubt that 'Mrs Heenan' was not all she claimed to be. Led by blunt allusions in the papers, scandal and gossip flourished. 'No actress,' protested Frank Queen loyally, 'has been more talked about, vilified and misrepresented.' Socially, it hurt, but it did Menken little harm professionally. Theatre-goers were no less eager to see Heenan's mistress than they had been to see his 'wife'. More worrying to the friends of the absent fighter was the damage the news might do his morale in England. Few doubted the 'Boy's' admiration for Menken, despite their squabbles. A conquest over Sayers, a hero's homecoming, money to throw about—such, it was predicted, would restore the strained relationship. But, if Heenan received word of the scandal before fighting, would the conquest, the hero's homecoming, materialize?

In fact, the revelation of Menken's bigamy was to shatter his illusions. Its impact, when it came, was indicated by the bitterness with which Heenan later renounced the actress in a letter to the *New York Herald*.

Adah Isaacs Menken has taken the liberty of coupling my name with hers. She and some of her friends have done so repeatedly before, with the object of attracting public sympathy, and for the purpose of involving me in newspaper controversy, thereby making capital in her profession, whatever that might be. I have heretofore carefully refrained from taking any notice . . . but publication . . . in the most widely circulated paper in the country, renders refutation an act of justice to myself and a duty to my friends. I therefore solemnly declare that I was never married to her, or to anyone else. I was never possessed of any of her means; and never, to my knowledge, received or spent a dollar of her money. In conclusion, I have only to say that I shall never again take any notice of this affair in any manner; and it is with great reluctance that I do so now.

That was to come. For the moment, the questions asked by Heenan's supporters were threefold. Would the news reach England before the fight? Could Cusick keep it from his man until their work was done? And, should Heenan learn the truth prior to fighting, what result might it have on his performance? His enemies were not in doubt. While his fans in the Exchange, and elsewhere, reflected pensively, Morrissey relished developments. So did 'Dad' Cunningham, a fellow gambler staked to profit by a Sayers win. According to a mutual friend, they packed for England in high spirits. 'Morrissey seemed uncommonly confident. He had, he asserted, ten thousand dollars which said that Heenan was beaten.'

14 Rustic Interlude

> *It was a pleasant enough spot, and seemed*
> *to invite wayfaring people, such as we were,*
> *to rest from the fatigues of the road. . . .*
> *After examining it for a considerable time*
> *Mr Petulengro said, 'I say, brother, that*
> *would be a nice place for a tussle!'*
>
> GEORGE BORROW

The two men had the railway compartment to themselves. One, well tailored, with an astrakhan collar to his overcoat, thumbed the pages of *Fraser's Magazine*. Beside him on the seat were a copy of *Bell's Life* and Ordnance Survey maps of Surrey and Hampshire. After a while, he put down the magazine and joined his companion in watching the passing countryside. The other, about seventy years of age—'a sage of venerable and hoary aspect'—sucked a carbonized pipe whose fumes mingled thickly with the smell of locomotive soot. Gideon and Tom Oliver, respectively excursion manager and fight commissary, were on reconnaissance.

The locality they had marked for exploration was that of Farnborough, a village in Hampshire. Its strategic situation seemed ideal. It lay remotely amid heathland, far from Winchester, the centre of the county constabulary. It was close to the Hampshire–Surrey boundary. The nearest town of significance, Farnham, was in Surrey, its police therefore having no relevance. Today, Aldershot, a few miles south of Farnborough, is an urban area, but then it was little more than a newly settled army camp, still in the process of replacing its tents with huts. The military was not hostile to the prize-ring. Indeed, the officers of Aldershot might subscribe to ringside tickets. Above all, Farnborough, despite its isolation, could be reached in about two hours by both the South Eastern and South Western railways, which operated stations near the village.

For the purpose of their outing, the two men were travelling from London by South Western and returning by South Eastern. Oliver, an old pug who had beaten men such as Ben Burn, Ned Painter and Jem Turner in his day, had pitched more prize-rings than he could recall. His eye for a site was infallible. Gideon felt confident of finding one. Fields and hamlets unfurled in the scudding smoke. Sheep fled as the train passed. Bullocks ogled. Here and there, a yokel, parcelled in sackcloth and strapping against the bite of late winter, looked up as suspiciously as the beasts. George III—'Farmer George' as his subjects had called him—would have discovered few innovations in the Victorian countryside.

By 1860, suburban and agricultural development had not tamed the southern counties as it would before the end of the century. Wild places still existed quite close to the cities. Among them, the great heaths of Surrey and Hampshire possessed a savage beauty. Gideon described the view as 'elementally appropriate to the pursuits of Mars'. From Woking to Heath End, from Hindhead to Hartford Bridge, acres of wild desolation threw up bracken and spiky gorse. From north-east to south-west ran a single major carriageway, the London to Winchester turnpike. Breaking the solitude were picturesque regions of fertility, watered by heath streams, speckled with hamlets. Such places, among them Farnborough, had changed little since William Cowper wrote of them.

Alighting at the South Western Railway's halt, the travellers inspected the adjacent land. Remarking 'one good pasture, somewhat spongey', they marched briskly down the narrow, tree-lined lane to the village. The village street curved sickle-fashion past a farm and small orchard, straightened again and led at length to a cluster of brick dwellings near the South Eastern's station. These dated from recent times. For the rest, cowstalls, barns, stables, cottages of mellow age composed the conglomerate. Socially and atmospherically, Farnborough was typical of many small places then vulnerable to prize-fight excursionists.

There were two inns. The Alma, named after the Crimean victory, kept a two-wheeler for hire and lodged the occasional traveller. The

Prince of Wales drew its custom mainly from the cottages. A few of the clients were remembered by George Bourne, a writer who knew the village in his childhood. There was Goodfellow, who had a strikingly bald crown, and Nat Attfield, a 'strange, straddling, much-afflicted man, notable for having got up again after the knell had been rung for him'. There was also Jim Watts, a messenger—once a carter at Smith's farm—who possessed such a large head that his tall beaver hat was reputed to hold a bushel. Watts was a regular drinking man, frequently a drunk one.

The village had one shop. Above its door was the message: *Susannah Smith, licensed to sell Tea, Coffee, Tobacco, Snuff, Vinegar and Soap.* Inside, a wooden counter and bench supported scales, biscuit tins, home-baked loaves, pats of farm butter, chunks of bacon. There was a coffee-mill, and a pair of steps to reach the shelves on the back wall. The shelves contained groceries of various kinds, glass jars of sweets, bunches of tallow candles, brushes and so on. A string bag, full of children's play-balls, hung from a low ceiling. The shop, with its strong, spicy odour, occupied the end of a low half-timbered building, Street Farm House, which confronted arrivals to the village like a guard-post. Through diamond-paned casements, the mistress of the farm, a grey-haired, bespectacled widow known as Grandma Smith, surveyed strangers with keen vigilance.

Every night, according to her grandson, the widow and her daughter Susannah barricaded the long parlour window facing the street, piling chairs on a table which stood under it. If the obstacles were not impenetrable, the clatter as they fell would warn the house of intruders. Such mistrustfulness, common among country people, was justified. A regular procession of migrants and vagrants tramped the countryside, many surviving by lawlessness. So-called mouchers roamed alone, or in ragged bands, scrounging, pilfering, seeking handouts by thinly veiled menaces. Many were strong men; some, criminals driven from the cities. It was not difficult for them to terrorize unpoliced hamlets.

To folk such as the Smiths, little good came from cities. Few rustics had seen a city; those who had, confirmed the worst. The most venturesome of Grandma Smith's offspring, her son Bill, recalled a visit to London where, in New Cut, a 'flimp' had snatched his handkerchief. Bill's cries of 'Stop, thief!' had produced nothing but laughter from the city crowd. The railways reinforced rural prejudice. For the Smiths, the arrival of the South Western line had meant a farm cut in two without compensation, and months in fear of the navvies who built the track. Protected by no more than a part-time constable, the neighbourhood had been invaded by a gang of brawny 'foreigners' who spent their free time spoiling for trouble. When they moved on, the best of the Smiths' pasture was destroyed, and a pit, dug to obtain ballast, marked the land like a wound. Local craftsmen soon suffered. Rail-freighted factory goods from London doomed many village industries, including a small pottery at Farnborough.

Strangers from 'the smoke' attracted black looks. From the dark windows of cottages, eyes swivelled suspiciously as the prize-fight scouts passed. Beneath the centrepiece of the street, an ancient elm, a group which had just witnessed the slaughter of a porker on a bed of straw glared dumbly at the visitors. At Smith's Farm, a black and white dog on a chain barked mistrustfully. Through a gate could be seen the archetypal English farmyard: 'a dirty duckpond, a stretch of slate-coloured mud with a grunting pig or two lying in it, cowstalls and cartsheds . . . filth trickling into a muckheap.' Hens scratched among rusty barrel-hoops. There was a water-tub and pigsties. Tom Oliver shook his head.

At the Alma, where the travellers refreshed themselves, discreet inquiries evinced guarded comment on the ownership of local land. The village had evolved its own tales to dissuade snoopers. It was hinted darkly that a dead farmer named Barnes frequented the meadows without a head. More hopefully, Gideon's map proclaimed a small stream, the Blackwater, defining the Hampshire–Surrey border at the far end of the village, near the South Eastern's station. Here, the stationmaster, one Grimstead, proved co-operative. Pointing across tousled meadows from the platform, he indicated the lie of the water, less a stream than a broad ditch.

Though several hedges and dykes intervened, accessibility was possible. The scouts found the grass on the banks flat and well drained. A line of trees formed a natural screen on one side. Tactically, it was good ground. With no more than an agile leap, a retreat from county to county could be achieved. 'Tom dug his heel in the turf, sucked his pipe, and looked satisfied.' The search was over. It remained to reach

Tom Sayers – statuette by Bezzi *(National Portrait Gallery, London)*

Heenan and Sayers fight for the first World Championship at Farnborough, Hampshire on April 17, 1860 *(Radio Times Hulton Picture Library)*

John Carmel Heenan, Menken's pugilist husband, sketched at the time of his famous battle with Tom Sayers for the World Championship *(Radio Times Hulton Picture Library)*

accommodation with the landlord, and swear him to secrecy. Dusk was closing as the travellers re-entrained. Oil lamps glimmered in windows, and the smoke of wood-fires hung over the village—the unsuspecting venue of the great fight.

*

From a railway standpoint, the situation was convenient, for the South Western's directors were reluctant to get involved. The company had already been indicted by Surrey magistrates for 'a misdemeanour at common law, in permitting certain trains to be run carrying passengers for the purpose of committing an illegal act [*prize-fighting*], and doing so for gain and reward by charging a special fare for such purpose'. It had taken considerable persuasion on the part of the company to convince the justices that the board of directors had known nothing of the operation, and was determined to prevent a repetition of it.

Smiles, of the South Eastern, was less perturbed by official ire. More than once in the past year, he had fobbed off complaints from the authorities with glib words. In April, the provision of a fight train on the Tonbridge–Ashford line had been the subject of a police report to the Home Office, and Smiles had had to plead ignorance. A few months later, a South Eastern fight excursion on the Tunbridge Wells–Hastings line brought a personal complaint from a Kent magistrate named Courthope to the Home Secretary. Courthope charged that, despite earlier assurances, the South Eastern had not only provided transport for the Fancy, but had actually hindered the police in their duties.

According to his testimony, an excursion train of thirty carriages, bearing fighters and spectators, had stopped on the open track between Ticehurst and Etchingham stations, disgorging into the countryside 'a large concourse of persons of a very questionable character, to the annoyance and disgust of respectable inhabitants'. Moreover, when a local police sergeant had asked the station master at Etchingham to transmit a call by railway telegraph for reinforcements, the station master had replied that the telegraph would not be available for some hours. Smiles, pressed by the Home Office for an explanation, was not lost. The alleged excursion train, he wrote, was actually a relief for the 6.30 a.m. from London Bridge—'an absolute necessity' due to the large number of people booked to Etchingham that morning. It was company policy, he added, to carry all ticket-holding passengers who arrived for advertised services.

Denying that the train had stopped between stations, Smiles claimed that it had only appeared to do so because its length, three hundred yards, could not be accommodated at a country halt. The front portion had been alongside the platform; the rest unavoidably extended from the station. As to the telegraph, station masters had instructions to transmit all messages in strict order of application, Smiles explained. At the time of the police request, there had already been thirty-seven messages awaiting transmission at Etchingham. The police call 'would have been transmitted in due course'. If this information can hardly have placated Justice Courthope, the Home Office let it go without protest. Unlike the South Western—and contrary to the understanding of *The Times*—the South Eastern Railway Company was quite prepared to do a deal on Farnborough.

15 A Trick Too Often

I can't but remember (tho' far apart now)
That we've met at a 'mill'—that we've shar'd in a row;
That over the bowl we've forgotten our woes,
Drank success to our friends, and reform to our foes
At many a scene of delight we have met,
That tho' sweet to remember, 'twere wise to forget.
WILLIAM LEMEN REDE

Jem Mace believed in fortune-telling. He had worked at fairs, and liked the Romanies. Could he have peered into a crystal ball in 1860, and seen himself five years ahead in the embrace of the most celebrated woman in London, he would have been amazed. He would have seen the 'star' dressing-room at Royal Astley's Amphitheatre, festooned with bouquets; tables littered with letters from admirers; a suite at the Westminster Palace Hotel which was lavish beyond his imagination. At the centre of the crystal ball was Adah Menken, at the height of her career as the 'Naked Lady'. Heenan was taking Mace to the show, taking him backstage, introducing him to the Louisiana seductress, who greeted the 'Boy' with condescension.

In the crystal, Menken was surrounded by devotees. She entertained them in two *salons*. Her hotel rooms were reserved chiefly for intellectual admirers; her rooms at the theatre, for the motley assortment of bucks and sporting men among whom she let her hair down. Mace and Heenan became regular visitors, flirting, joking, consuming the liquor on her sideboard. Menken played with their affections. In a letter to Edwin James, she would write of Heenan in the mid-sixties:

> The dear Boy is very kind, very fond to [*sic*] me. . . . I know, and perhaps you do, that he never loved anybody but me. He never will.

There is only one love to one life. But it is too late . . . I can never be what I was once to him: truthful, pure and good. He destroyed a beautiful and bountiful nature. He seeks to restore that which is dead. Now, Ed., it is my turn to inflict suffering. I do not mean to hurt the only man I ever really cared for, but I cannot help it.

In the crystal, Menken flaunted her success and intimacy with other men in Heenan's face. To the initial embarrassment but growing pleasure of Mace, who had become the 'Boy's' close companion, she singled him out for partiality. Romantically inclined, and flattered, the English bruiser responded eagerly. In 1860, it would have seemed a fantasy. But it was in the crystal. Her hands caressing him. Her lips speaking privately in his ear. Her eyes watching Heenan maliciously. . . .

*

Heenan first met Jem Mace while training for the Sayers fight. Rather more than half-way through the build-up, towards the end of February, Macdonald suggested that the American should attend a British contest to familiarize himself with the atmosphere. Mace was due to fight a fancied boxer named Bob Travers. The excursion, starting from London and continuing by river, was convenient for Heenan, and Cusick did not object. On 21 February, the American champion, concealed from official eyes in a high-collared overcoat and a sealskin cap whose flaps enveloped his ears and cheeks, boarded the steamer *City of Rochester* with the fight crowd. On the trip, he met the combatants.

He found Mace an engaging, dark-eyed man of quick moods. Born at Beeston, Norfolk, twenty-nine years earlier, he had been the owner of a travelling boxing-booth before taking to the prize-ring at twenty-four. Between fights, he managed the Swan Inn, at Norwich. His form, exemplified by the whirlwind demolition of Posh Price and lame submission to Brettle, was erratic. Mace was unpredictable. At Gravesend, in '57, he had refused to fight because he did not like the referee. A year later, matched with a veteran bruiser named Mike Madden, he had arrived at Shoreditch rail terminus as appointed, ignored the excursion and, to the amazement of the Fancy, calmly boarded a train back to Norfolk. His behaviour inspired charges of duplicity and cowardice, but Heenan took to him.

Mace's opponent, Bob Travers, was an accomplished black fighter with victories over such established middleweights as Madden, Jesse Hatton, George Crockett and Bill Hayes. Then managed by Nat Langham, Travers was strongly influenced by the evasive technique that had enabled Langham to survive against Sayers, a factor of special interest to the 'Benicia Boy'. Travers was a master at out-staying his adversaries. Twice, he had fought for well over three hours; once, against Hayes, for almost four hours. A cheerful fellow, with a broad grin, he was a good draw. Henry Miles referred to him fondly as 'Massa Ebony'.

If Heenan, now the centre of attention, had looked forward to a restful break from training, the outing failed to meet his hopes. After a bracing voyage in the estuary, combatants and followers disembarked at a quiet spot on the Essex coast, only to find that the law had been forewarned. No sooner was the ring pitched than cries of 'Crushers!' and 'Miltonians!' scattered the Fancy in confusion. Macdonald, mindful of the consequences should Heenan be arrested at a prize-fight, told the American to run for it. Around them, spectators were scrambling for the landing boats with 'Olympian agility'. Heenan reached the nearest craft ahead of the constables and was helped aboard by an arm which he found, on taking stock, to be that of Mace.

It was a hectic day. At about 4 p.m., diverted to the coast of Kent, the steamer put its passengers down again. This time, the fight was started, but had got no further than six rounds when a mass of blue uniforms appeared at the ringside. Taking advantage of the Fancy's preoccupation, the Kent police had moved in undetected, and now attempted to apprehend the principals. In this, the officers were unsuccessful, though Travers was lucky to squirm free from the assailants. Heenan, once more reaching safety on the steamer, watched one of the seconds, Jerry Noon, in flight from a hefty constable. Both were waist-deep in the sea before Noon, to the delight of those already on the ship, shed his jacket and swam to freedom. A whip-round was held on deck to buy him some new clothes. By dusk, the fight postponed until the morning, Heenan had seen something of the hazards encountered at British sporting venues.

Next day, he re-embarked for a more successful outing. The police, perhaps underestimating the persistence of the Fancy, were not seen, and the contest ran its full course. Though unmemorable as a tussle, it was in one feature significant, not least in relation to Heenan's plans. Travers stripped in impressive shape. With his glossy lines went a supple action at variance with the stiffer orthodoxy of Mace, who soon dispelled doubts as to his earnestness. 'After a little sparring, Mace got home beautifully on Bob's black-letter title-page. When Travers retreated, hitting out, Mace followed. Bob paused a moment, then rushed in hand-over-hand. Mace planted his left with fine judgement, following it with a jab from the right. There was some fibbing in the close, and both went down by the ropes.' Travers had seen enough to discount an easy victory. Settling for Nat Langham's strategy, he began provoking Mace with sudden flurries, letting his opponent work, and getting down to avoid harm. It might have been an arranged demonstration for Heenan, who was shown a perfect exhibition of the process by which Langham had beaten Sayers.

Greater interest was to follow. Angered by the falls which repeatedly cheated Mace's best attacks, his seconds, Bos Tyler and Jack Hicks, persistently complained of a breach of regulations. Their supporters joined in barracking the umpires. At the end of the third round, Tyler appealed firmly to the referee, who ordered, 'Carry on.' In the fourth, there were chants of 'Remember the thirteenth rule!' (i.e., *That it shall be a fair stand-up fight, and if either man shall wilfully throw himself down without receiving a blow, whether blows shall have previously been exchanged or not, he shall be deemed to have lost the encounter*). The normal laxity in enforcing the rule was being stubbornly challenged. A few rounds later, when Hicks protested, Travers was cautioned. Encouraged, Mace's partisans howled louder at every fall. At last, the referee was sufficiently concerned to enter the ring and warn Travers of the risk he was incurring.

Smilingly, Travers blamed the turf for his tumbles. It was the customary excuse, accompanied by a round or two of compliance before the tactic was re-employed. Neither he nor Langham took the warning very seriously. Soon, he was back at the old game, teasing and tumbling through another dozen rounds or so. Mace's fans were now barely restrained by the ring-keepers. For ninety minutes they had watched Travers blatantly flout the rule while the referee procrastinated. Travers's friends supported him vociferously. It was an unenviable situation for a referee, whose decision to stop a fight might precipitate pitched battle. But, in the ninety-first minute, it was taken. Catching Mace with a smart cut, Travers, now indifferent to rebuke, got down to avoid retaliation. This time, the referee did not equivocate. The offender was disqualified.

Uproar was immediate. In what a bystander described as 'a scene of disgraceful confusion', the loser's friends 'assailed the referee with the foulest abuse, refusing to accept his decision. Travers, shedding tears, declared his readiness to fight on, but never to shake hands with his opponent.' The dispute did not end on the battlefield. For several days, acrimonious correspondence sought to stop the stakeholder paying out, its extent and virulence testifying to the shock of the ruling. When it was finally announced that the stakeholder had ratified Jem Mace's victory, a new complexion had been placed on fight strategy. If Travers had cause for reflection, so did Sayers. Warning had been served that the falling game could not be played with impunity.

16 Come and Join Us

His hat was like a funeral, he'd got a waiter's coat,
With a hallelujah collar and a choker round his throat,
His pals would laugh and say in chaff that Bendigo was right
In taking on the devil, since he'd no one else to fight.

SIR ARTHUR CONAN DOYLE

Police duty in Southwark, the turbulent Thames-side district between Blackfriars and London Bridge, inured a constable to life's seamy aspects. The lurid reputation of the area dated from medieval times, when it was known as Stewsbank. Until the reign of Henry VIII, protected brothels, leased from the clergy, had abounded between Bear Gardens and Clink Street, east of Skin Market. In the 'Cross Bones', at Park Street, lay the unconsecrated remains of prostitutes from some eighteen houses licensed by bishops. Nearby was Dead Man's Place—so-called for the corpses dumped there in the great plague—and Shakespeare's Maid Lane. More recently, Barclay and Perkins's brewery had smothered the site of the Globe and Hope theatres, the second a prize-fight arena in its later days. Bear-baiting, once a feature of the district, had died out. Dog-fighting, rioting, vice and crime remained in Southwark.

Symbolic of the new age and its rapacious thirst, the brick palace of Barclay and Perkins had risen like a Phoenix from the ashes of an earlier company, Thrale's brewery, which had burned down in 1822. Samuel Johnson, executor of Thrale's will, placed the business on the market with prophetic words: 'We are not here to sell a parcel of boilers and vats, but the potentiality of growing rich beyond the dreams of avarice.' Messrs Barclay and Perkins saw the truth of Johnson's message. By the middle of the century, the malodorous monster overshadowing the slums of Southwark was so noted a landmark that at least one prominent visitor to London called there in preference to Westminster or St Paul's.

At the peak of his achievement as Austria's supremo, Baron von Haynau armed himself with an introduction from the Rothschilds and arrived to watch Englishmen brewing beer. Unfortunately for Haynau, whose repressions in Hungary were well known, the Southwarkians were crudely irrepressible. Cursing him as a tyrant and murderer, one grabbed his large moustache while an angry crowd beat him with fists and sticks. Haynau was stupefied. Breaking free, he fled to the river pursued by draymen, coal-heavers and labourers.

'He ran in a frantic manner along Bankside,' reported *The Times*, 'until he came to the George public house, when, forcing the door open, he rushed in and proceeded upstairs to one of the bedrooms, to the utter astonishment of Mrs Benfield, the landlady. . . . The furious mob rushed in after him, threatening to do for "the Austrian butcher", but the house is very old fashioned and contains a vast number of doors, which were all forced open except that of the room in which the general had hidden.'

Appalled to find her premises surrounded by a crowd several hundred strong, landlady Benfield sent word to Southwark police station, where the officer in charge, Inspector Squires, assembled a detail and marched stoically to the George. It was a brave act. The Southwarkians were not respectful of uniforms. The inspector's men still smarted from the bricks hurled at them by a hostile crowd when they had entered the slums to arrest a counterfeiter named Morris. Now, shouldering their way to the public house, Squires and his constables hustled the baron to the river steps, bundled him into a police boat and, amid the execrations of a cheated mob, conveyed him to the north bank.

Such were the hazards of law-enforcement in the neighbourhood. Neither Squires nor those who followed him were easily ruffled by exigencies. When, at the end of February 1860, it was reported that a number of bruisers and sporting roughs were converging on a revivalist rally in the Park Street area, the constabulary mounted solid but tactful observation. Evangelism was in full flood in London. William Booth, founder of the Salvation Army, was preaching regularly with the Methodist New Connection. That year his wife, Catharine, began her women's ministry. In Southwark, Charles Haddon Spurgeon, the former boy preacher from Kelvedon, Essex, was attracting such large crowds that his Park Street chapel could not contain the numbers. His sermons, set in print, sold literally by the ton.

It was strong stuff. Spurgeon pitched his puritan message unsparingly at the emotions; Booth promised eternal punishment to the unconverted. Their congregations were not the meek of the city. Behind the thumping mission bands followed cabmen, costers, dockers—'rough diamonds' whose revivalist activities were often as troublesome to the police as less inspired breaches of the public peace. Increasingly, the spiritual and the sporting spheres conflicted. The Reverend Joshua Cautley of Broughton, Bedfordshire, not only cut the ropes at a prize-fight, but attempted to exercise his citizen's power of arrest on a pugilist. He was joined in a rowdy scene by the Reverend Edward Orlebar Smith, another Bedfordshire cleric. John Bright, the radical Quaker and orator from Rochdale, was tireless in denouncing 'the brutalities of prize-fighters'.

Bright's chief publishing medium, the *Morning Star*, condemned the prize-ring but printed full reports of its proceedings. Less businesslike, the short-lived *Dial* pursued its aim of 'purifying the daily Press' by excluding from its columns not only boxing items but all 'so-called sporting news'. Thus, the lines of conscience were drawn and manned. Passion was not entirely with the moralists. There were men who genuinely held fist-fighting a force for good. 'As a mode of settling differences,' wrote Dowling, 'and more especially among the humbler ranks of society, it is at once manly and praiseworthy, a fit and humane substitute for those savage practices to which men in a barbarous state too frequently have recourse. . . . It teaches men to rely on those powers with which Nature has imbued them . . . it promotes that indomitable bravery which, whenever and wherever called into action, had distinguished the character of Englishmen all over the globe. It represses those treacherous and cowardly propensities which, in countries where boxing is unknown, lead to the use of the knife and stiletto.'

To Henry Miles, as to battling Bill Doherty later, the knuckle game was 'a thing kindly and lovable', even in its way sacred. According to Miles, 'a wave of cant was sweeping the country'. The result, he feared, was an age 'when even the first principles of fair-play to an antagonist, and forbearance towards the vanquished, seem to be fast vanishing out of the minds of a pusillanimous populace'. Doubtless, the constables of Southwark had their own views. But it was no part of police duty to take sides. Their role in Park Street was a watching brief with partiality only for law and order.

News that unfamiliar customers of a muscular stamp, disfigured by the 'thick ears, bubukles, knobs and whelks' of the fighting breed, had appeared in the George and the near-by Anchor tavern, departing with self-conscious sobriety at the call of the mission drum, could not be ignored by the Southwark 'blues'. Bruisers were associated in the district with a number of activities, from mugging to 'bouncing' at brothels and low gaffs. Religious communion was not one of those activities. The strained air they wore amid the faithful converging on the concourse, the awkward way they hung back on the fringes, fingering their coloured neckerchiefs, betrayed their embarrassment. To the constables on duty, the presence of such unlikely repenters was mysterious, if not ominous. Word of Bendigo's appearance had not reached the officers.

A decade after his retirement, the celebrated Midlander had acquired a comfortable spread under his velveteen waistcoat; a genial, florid face. True, he had yet to embrace reform whole-heartedly. In '59, Bendigo had accepted training commissions to pay for the liquor he still consumed on occasions with unfortunate consequences. But he was mellowing. The spiritual disposition of the Thompsons was astir in him. Later assertions that he followed his kinsmen in the Methodist ministry are improbable—age and illiteracy would have barred his adoption—but the repute he achieved as a speaker at London's nonconformist missions, notably at King's Cross and Holborn Circus, was unquestionable. By patient listening, he came in time to know much of the Bible. It pleased him to draw personal parallels. Reflecting on the fishermen of Galilee and the left-handed warriors of Gibeah, Bendigo declared artlessly: '*I've* won a lot of fishing prizes with the rod Mr Walter of *The Times* gave me . . . and *I'm* left-handed. It was being left-handed as took in the clever ones I fought against.'

Bendigo had come south more than once in the past year, and had many friends in London. He was accompanied on his latest trip from

Nottingham by an older brother, an ardent revivalist, and a number of converts bearing testimony to Southwark. According to pub legend, his promise to address the faithful was dismissed as a joke by many sporting men; others, putting nothing past 'Bendy', found the prospect irresistible. They were not, it seems, cheated. Introduced as 'a soul in search of salvation', Bendigo purportedly received a good reception from the gathering. The tale stops short of his actual declaration, but, since his platform repertoire was limited, an address recorded later at the Cabmen's Mission, King's Cross, may be admissible. Bendigo, claiming his salvation 'a miracle', made a touching appeal to public sentiment:

'What could I do? I was the youngest born of twenty-one children, and the first thing they did with me was put me in the workhouse. There I got among fellows that brought me out. I became a fighting character. . . . I came to London to fight Ben Caunt, and licked him. . . . I didn't think I should ever come to London to fight for Jesus. But here I am. I wish I could read out of the Blessed Book, then I could talk to you better. But I never learned to read, though I'm hoping by listening to pick up more of the Bible, then I'll talk to you better. . . . I've got a lot of cups and trophies which I won when I was fighting. Them cups and trophies will fade. But there's a crown being fashioned for old Bendigo that will never fade.'

That it sounded remarkably like a plea for mitigation was reasonable. Bendigo's talents as a speaker had been practised chiefly from the dock in police courts. None the less, the congregation was much moved. On the evidence of Henry Lucy, a writer who was present, a hymn was sung for the convert: *Praise God from whom all blessings flow; Praise Him for brother Bendigo.* At Southwark, the meeting dispersed in contented mood. Streaming homeward by ferry to Charing Cross, by London Bridge, or southward to Newington, the crowds displayed a humour entirely pleasing to the constables. If a frivolous newspaper comment can be believed, the only untoward incident at the gathering had come when a preacher 'besought the flock to fight the good fight. A gentleman of robust appearance bestirred himself at the back. "Leave that to Tom Sayers!" he shouted.'

17 Words in Parliament

MY DEAR MR PUNCH . . . *They ought to have*
been both taken up, and put into prison,
and done . . . And I think gentlemen ought to
be ashamed of themselves to encourage such
savages to bruise and hurt one another.
Talk of cruel sports . . . Ever your affectionate,

EMILY.
Punch

In April, American newspaper correspondents in London reported the imminence of the title fight. The *New York Herald*'s man in England wrote:

The match has finally been fixed for Tuesday, the 17th of April. The tickets are not yet issued, nor is it generally known that the day has been settled. The stakeholder professes not to know himself where the fight will take place. . . . An impression is being circulated with a view, I think, to put the police off the scent, that the mill will come off at a great distance from London. It is my opinion, however, that it will be very near here, and that it will take place in private grounds.

Dealing with public reaction, the writer added:

Up to this time, the English people scarcely know what to think of the boldness of Heenan in crossing the Atlantic to fight with the champion of Britain, the hero of a dozen fights, who never was beaten but once. They say that Heenan must either be very soft-headed, or must have some good reason to believe he will be successful. No one seems to doubt that the whole thing is fair and square; and although, as a matter of pride, most of the natives are in favor of Sayers, the motto 'May the best man win' is very generally echoed. For the last fortnight, betting has been seven to four on Sayers, though a few small sums have been laid at two to one.

Of course, it is impossible to be very accurate in such a supposition, but a gentleman well posted in sporting circles tells me that he thinks at least a hundred thousand pounds will change hands in England on the result of the fight. Sporting men believe it will be a short one, but that if it lasts over half an hour Sayers's advantage will diminish due to the 'Boy's' superior size, weight and reach. Still, with two such hard hitters, a chance blow may decide the matter at an early stage.

Since the legal proceedings against Heenan in Derby, the fight organizers had been 'very careful and shy about giving any information which might, by leaking out, aid the police and magisterial authorities in the determined effort they are making to prevent the fight'. An approximate schedule, for travel purposes, had been released, but only to New York. Confidentially, the American press was informed that tickets would be on sale in London on the evening of Monday, 16 April, and that a rail excursion would leave the city before daylight. The best advice *Sporting Life* could offer home enthusiasts was that:

Those who have made up their minds to be present at the mill must keep their weather eye open, and be in readiness for a tremendous journey, and we should advise all such to be especially on the alert during Sunday and Monday next, for they will have to be prepared for any emergency which may arise. The spot which has been selected, it is supposed, will be impregnable to the attacks of the police, whose right to enter private property will be resisted in the most positive manner, not only on reasonable but on legal grounds. The *Sporting Life* will be fully represented, and it is only just to those who have the management of the affair to state that they are determined to afford us every facility for obtaining the most complete report of the encounter.

Reduced to guess-work, London waited until the second week of April, when the influx of visitors from the United States plainly marked the approach of the contest. In the West End, hotels such as Morley's, Osborne's, Stone's, Bunyard's and the Westminster Palace were packed with Americans. Scores of transatlantic sportsmen and gamblers strolled the streets, sampling entertainments, visiting 'tourist spots'. The phenomenon was unique. Knowledge of departure dates—a number of the visitors were known to be booked on the *Vanderbilt*, which sailed from Southampton on the 18th—clearly placed the fight within a few days.

Little else held any interest in the pubs, clubs and divans. Excitement, observed a British reporter, diverted 'all England from its normal business'. Parliament was not excluded. On 13 April, a member named Hadfield called the attention of the Government to what he described as 'a meditated breach of the peace by a pugilistic contest to take place between an American citizen and a British subject for a so-called championship'. Hadfield, claiming that newspapers had given notice of the time and place, demanded of the Home Secretary 'whether he intended to take measures to put down this projected disturbance of the public peace and prevent an exhibition contrary to the religious sense of the country'. Could the nation, he insisted, rely on the Home Secretary to prevent so brutal and demoralizing an exhibition to the rising generation? The question raised laughter on several sides.

In reply, the Home Secretary, Sir George Cornewall Lewis, said that the contest had been brought to his notice, and that he had no doubt the Commissioner of Police would 'take the necessary steps to prevent a breach of peace within the metropolitan district. Beyond this I cannot assure my honourable friend. I cannot venture to give any positive promise, for if he is informed of the time and place, I am not. I don't think they are fixed. It is, therefore, impossible for me to say whether the police will succeed in preventing the incursion in question.' This satisfied neither Hadfield nor, among others, Lord Lovaine, who was particularly dissatisfied with the Government's failure to stop the letting of trains for fight excursions.

Pursuing the issue at a later time, Lovaine pressed the premier, Lord Palmerston, on his attitude, branding him as a fan of the knuckle game.

Scarcely discomforted by the recommendation, the premier preened his side-whiskers. Though too prudent to be seen at prize-fights, Palmerston had a shrewd appreciation of the traditional British feeling for robust sports. His fondness of the field, especially racing, was no secret. That year, his horse Mainstone was to be Derby favourite, and his trainer, John Day, was known to visit Westminster for racing talks. It was a familiar ploy among cartoonists to depict the premier as a pugilist, squaring up to his political opponents. He addressed Lovaine on the subject with urbanity:

> I would not contest the technical question that a fight between two men—not a fight of enmity, but a trial of strength—is, legally, a breach of peace, and an act that renders the parties liable to prosecution; nor that the persons who go to witness it are, technically, involved in the charge. But, as far as they are concerned, they may conceive it to be a very harmless pursuit. Some persons like what takes place, though there may be a difference of opinion, as a matter of taste, whether it is a spectacle one would wish to see, or whether it is calculated to excite disgust. Some people look upon it as an exhibition of manly courage, characteristic of the people of this country . . . this is, of course, entirely a matter of opinion. But really, setting aside legal technicalities, I do not perceive why any number of persons who assemble to witness a prize-fight are, in their own persons, more guilty of a breach of peace than an equal number of persons who assemble to witness a balloon ascent.

Encouraged by appreciative laughter, Palmerston capped the point:

> There they stand; there is no breach of the peace; they go to see a sight, and when that sight is over they return, and no injury is done to anyone. They only sit or stand on the grass to witness the performance—and as to the danger to those who perform, I imagine the risk to life in the case of those who go up in balloons is certainly greater than that of those who merely hit each other without inflicting permanent injury. I think there is a moderate path in all things, in all opinions; and although it may or may not be desirable that the law should be enforced—whatever the law may be—still I do not think any advantage is gained or good done, either to public morals

or public feeling, by the sort of exaggerations put forward by the opponents of prize-fighting.

On the opposition benches, Colonel Dickson, a gusty warrior, rose to support the premier. Confirming that he sat on a different side of the House from the noble lord, and did not often find himself in the same lobby, Dickson felt compelled to say of the Prime Minister that if he had one attribute more than another which endeared him to his countrymen it was his thoroughly English character 'and his love for every manly sport'. Amid applause, the colonel condemned any legislative attempt to stop 'manly sports'. On the duties of magistrates, the law was clear, he said. 'Magistrates ought to know when to act and when to shut their eyes.'

Unfortunately, as some in the wider world saw it, the rule of English magistrates for some months had been to act with vigour against Heenan and shut their eyes to Sayers. Aware of American disgruntlement, the British camp was at pains to inform correspondents of its disgust at all harassment. 'Sayers has conveyed a message to us expressing his annoyance at the treatment Heenan has received,' declared one New York journalist, 'and tendering him his warmest sympathy.'

In fact, Heenan—'extremely confident and in high spirits'—appears to have flourished on molestation, and the public support that it gained for him. Ironically, the one surprise which upset his good temper came in the last days of training, when Cusick and Macdonald had successfully secreted him from the law. Opening the latest papers to reach England from New York, Heenan was astounded to read the revelations of Alexander Menken. To Cusick, they betokened unimaginable mischief, beyond even the woman of his nightmares. Yet events were to modify his first alarm, for, exercised by anger, the 'Boy' worked with notably less complacence than hitherto. 'He hit the punchbag as if he really meant it,' Macdonald said.

Drama had not entirely missed the other camp. Resigned, unlike Heenan, to domestic compromise, Sayers faced a new liability in 1860. That year, his wife conceived her third child by Alfred Aldridge— the future Charles Aldridge Sayers—staking one more future on the coming fight. Already supporting Sarah's extravagances and four expensive children, two of them Aldridge's, the champion's burden was onerous. At thirty-four, he badly needed the profits of victory, the belt that would guarantee prestige in retirement. He was running out of fighting years. As just another beaten champion, he would be grimly placed. Tom Sayers had known economic desperation in the past—but not with five children to feed, clothe and educate.

April brought him an unexpected ally. In March, Bob Fuller, the pedestrian, had joined him at Newmarket. Now, a posse of strangers arrived in camp, led by a bear-like figure with a dense beard and a fur coat which fell to his ankles. 'Old Smokey' had come to give his advice. With him were 'Dad' Cunningham and two cronies from Troy, Morrissey's hometown: John Lawrence and Morris Barron. All were eager to see Heenan beaten. Whether Morrissey's tactical counsel was valid is problematical. The 'Benicia Boy' he had stopped at Long Point had been unfit and overweight; a different proposition from the athlete now in training. But, at least psychologically, Sayers gained by the company of Morrissey. The brash confidence of the flamboyant American topped morale in the British camp with a gaudy crown. Proclaimed *Sporting Life* in its last issue before the fight:

> Tom Sayers's condition is perfection. During the week he has been taking his breathings on Newmarket Heath, and the indefatigable Bob Fuller never loses sight of him. Harry Brunton has, as usual, been with the champion, giving him the finishing touches. Tom looks superb. His eye is as bright as a star; his complexion as clear as alabaster. Stripped, he looks better than ever in his life, and his muscles are as hard as iron. Last week he visited the race course at Newmarket, and was admired by everyone. Dressed in a fashionable suit, he strolled about the heath with Fuller, Morrissey and Brunton. The champion is as confident as if Heenan's sponge were already thrown up. . . .
>
> At the same time, he has decided not to hold Benicia's Child too cheap, and will miss no opportunity of obtaining the honour of an early and decided victory. Heenan's party are equally satisfied with their man. Notwithstanding the vexatious difficulties with which he has been surrounded, he is now going on as well as his partisans can desire. He will enter the ring ready to fight for his very life.

III AND THE JAWS CRACKLE

Their flying Fists around the Temples glow,
And the Jaws crackle with the massy Blow

PAUL WHITEHEAD

18 The Eve of Battle

London Town's a dashing place
For ev'ry thing that's going,
There's fun and gig in ev'ry face,
So natty and so knowing
PIERCE EGAN

Throughout Monday, April 16, the Fancy streamed into London by train and road from all over the country. *Bell's Life* of Sunday morning had listed the places in the capital where excursion tickets would be available Monday evening. Including Owen Swift's Horseshoe, Tichbourne Street; Nat Langham's Cambrian, Castle Street; George Bryer's Black Horse, Oxenden Street; and Harry Brunton's George and Dragon, Barbican, the ticket parlours became increasingly crowded as the day progressed.

The George and Dragon was the scene of exceptional excitement, for Brunton had returned to the pub from Newmarket, bringing Morrissey to stay with him. Many who thronged the selling houses were Americans, savouring the atmosphere of the English tap-room. 'The parlour was filled with queer-looking men drinking ale, smoking bad tobacco and speculating on the result of the morrow,' wrote a New Yorker of the George and Dragon. 'Outside, a crowd of small boys seemed firmly to believe that Sayers and Heenan were then and there about to put their differences to the test.' Strangers stopped each other on the pavement asking for news of the arrangements.

Beset by rumours, much of the city passed the day in confusion about the fight. Enterprising pedlars sold worthless tickets to the gullible, and at least one publisher put criers on the streets with an 'extra' announcing that the battle was over and that Heenan had been whipped. There was no shortage of greenhorns to snap it up.

Everywhere, the contest was a major topic, and many arguments flared between partisans. In the afternoon, the correspondent of the *New York Herald* accompanied a friend to a bootmaker in the Strand, to make a purchase. The proprietor immediately engaged them in fight talk.

'He had taken us for Englishmen, and in the course of his remarks expressed the patriotic, though somewhat sanguinary wish that "Sayers would whip every drop of blood out of Heenan's body". My friend demurred to this, and after a lively altercation we left the establishment without giving an order for the boots we wanted.'

As evening approached, opinion in the flash taverns and other points of congregation consolidated in favour of a Sayers victory. Betting moved generally to 2 to 1, with a few offers at 3 to 1. Morrissey exerted a strong influence on prices. According to one reporter, 'his biased opinions and expressions had affected the confidence even of Heenan's friends'. More convincingly, perhaps, he backed his assertions with substantial sums of money—reputedly more than a thousand pounds in all, on Sayers. In the late afternoon, Morrissey and Cunningham joined Bob Brettle, Ben Caunt, 'Slasher' Perry, and a number of other veteran bruisers, in Owen Swift's ale room. Something like a hundred enthusiasts jammed the place to catch a glimpse of them.

The crush inside was exceeded only by the scramble outside. A London journalist, arriving for a ticket, found the crowd seeking admission 'overwhelming and impossible to break through . . . we waited patiently until the living current pushed us forward'. Demand for tickets was not confined to the regular Fancy. Besides the customary throng of hardened punters, of costermongers, wealthy ne'er-do-wells and sporting toughs, were 'members of both Houses of Parliament in plenty. Authors, poets, painters, soldiers, and even clergymen were present'.

So many of the nobility sought to attend the fight that one, the Earl of Eglinton and Winton, actually felt obliged to write to the papers disclaiming his interest. Another who later disclaimed involvement, though less convincingly, was the poet Thackeray, whose accounts of the contest were resoundingly firsthand. Charles Dickens, then editor of the magazine *All the Year Round*, obtained a ticket. Dickens was no sportsman. His admission of the fact in the preface to the *Pickwick Papers* was corroborated by his description of the cricket match at Dingley Dell and his portrait, in *Dombey and Son*, of the 'Game Chicken'. But he was interested in violence of many forms. His intention to attend the fight was circumvented at a late hour, and he delegated the assignation to a fellow journalist, John Hollingshead.

The sale of tickets began after dark. By now, the crowds outside the advertised taverns were inclined to be unruly, and it was seen as a nice touch when policemen on patrol in the streets helped to keep order and expedite the passage of clients through the doors. The tickets themselves advised no destination. *Return journey to London* and *London to* —— was roughly stamped on red, white and blue card. Selling at three guineas—about six times the normal third-class fare for the round trip—these passports were beyond the means of most labourers, and, it was hoped, of the hooligan elements. Having paid for his ticket, the purchaser was instructed to be at London Bridge rail terminus, ready to entrain, by four o'clock in the morning.

While many ticket-holders retired for some early rest, the remainder of the Fancy, including Americans, settled for a night of entertainment. The sporting pubs soon became centres of carousing. Elsewhere, the names of Heenan and Sayers were on all lips. In music halls, cheap gaffs and suck-cribs (beer shops), wherever men of fighting interest met, the talk was of form and betting prices. Anecdotes of legendary battles were recalled. How Mendoza the Jew had given 'Gentleman' Dick Humphries the fight of his violent life. How the battered wreck of Hen Pearce, the 'Game Chicken', had heaved itself from the turf to deliver the blow that robbed John Gully of the championship. How Tom Cribb had been allowed to get up and beat Black Molyneux after lying unconscious a full minute at the Negro's feet.

It was a fine evening, and the pleasures of the West End beckoned. At the Royal Princess's Theatre that week, Louise Keeley was playing in *My Wife's Out*. The Royal Strand Theatre offered *The Miller and His Men* and *Caught by the Ears*. More demurely, *The Pilgrim of Love*, 'a new fairy romance', attracted playgoers to the Haymarket's Theatre Royal. At Astley's Royal Amphitheatre, Westminster Bridge Road, the provincial Fancy could take in London's latest spectacle, 'an equestrian version of the campaigns of Napoleon in Italy, Egypt and Russia'. Part circus, part theatre, Astley's included in its pageant

'Mademoiselle Mathilde riding a horse which upsets eight chairs in succession, then sets them up again, and a dwarf named Jonathan Jack who rides horseback with his legs crossed in front of him'.

There was no shortage of night-spots willing to relieve visitors of their cash. 'Our English host introduced us to several elegant houses,' wrote an American, 'where the female company was as agreeable as it was expensive.' At supper haunts such as Kellner's, in Leicester Square, and Evan's, in Covent Garden, there was cabaret, a smart ambience and fast women. At the Garrick's Head, off Bow Street, a well lined wallet could buy supper and breakfast for a partner who was willing to share the time in between. For dancers, there was the opulent Mott's, the livelier Argyll Rooms in the Haymarket, or the Holborn Casino—'glittering with a myriad prisms'—a popular hall renowned for easy pick-ups. No respectable woman frequented these places, but others, both amateur and professional, abounded.

When the theatres had closed, when the strains of polka and quadrille had faded, it was time to move to premises which defied normal licensing regulations. Such establishments were tucked away down guarded alleys of the type which led from Princess Street to Kate Hamilton's. Kate's place, near Leicester Square, came to life in the early hours, when its ornate mirrors reflected shimmering glass lustres, white waistcoats, soft female shoulders, champagne bottles and fine cigars. Here, the price of both drinks and whores was exorbitant. Young toffs lounged against the walls, or eyed the inviting décolletage of the prey from plush benches.

Kate, holding court from a throne-like pedestal at one end of the room, had a spry welcome for well breeched Americans, as for other out-of-town customers. According to Kellow Chesney, the authority on Victorian low-life, 'Mrs Hamilton, who presided, was a mountain of a woman, hideously ugly but with one of those mysterious talents for promoting "atmosphere". From midnight on she sat swigging champagne, now and then shaking with laughter like a gigantic blancmange.'

Outside, in the maze of shadowy courts and alleys between Leicester Square and the Haymarket, off Regent and Windmill Streets, the night-owls of the Fancy prowled the black heart of Babylon, a realm of temptation 'where rouge-caked drabs, unshaven bullies and prize-ring touts, bawds, swells in starched fronts and opera hats, and elegant women in yards of watered silk, were to be seen cheek by jowl. Here,' wrote Chesney, 'were squalid and dangerous criminal taverns like the notorious Black Bull, and high-class "night houses" bright with cut glass and staffed with liveried waiters.' Gradually the streets emptied. By two o'clock, most of the morning excursionists were catching a nap in preparation for an early start.

To the north, the Adam and Eve and the Green Man were shuttered, last tankards drained to Tom Sayers. To the south, tomorrow's brew lay heavy in the darkened vats of Barclay and Perkins, and the landlady of the George had rung out her bar cloths. On the riverside, a black forest of masts swayed above the shacks and pubs of Shadwell and Limehouse. Stars shone in a clear sky. The river ran silently.

Distantly, as in a dream, a restless sleeper in Walworth or Kennington might have heard the clatter of hooves and boots, and imagined a regiment on the move. Peering from his curtains, he might further have discerned the glint of cutlasses, the shape of domed helmets and belted coats. The forces passing in the night were not soldiers but policemen. Mayne's detectives had done their work. From Southwark, Newington, and other metropolitan depots, mounted and foot police were heading in strength for predetermined battle lines.

19 'Faust Flight'

The Beaks and Blues were watching
Agog to stop the mill,
As we gathered at the station
In the April morning chill;
By twos and threes, by fours and tens,
To London Bridge we drew;
For we had had 'the office'
Who were good men and true
W. M. THACKERAY (attrib.)

It was about three in the morning when the West End hotels saw the departure of their fight-bound visitors. Recalled one journalist: 'A pretty English chambermaid awoke us from a short doze. We were already prepared at a moment's notice, so we descended to the coffee room and, after receiving some refreshments, entered a hansom and pushed toward London Bridge. The shops along our route were closed. All the population had vacated the streets. A few gaslights glimmered, but the city seemed a graveyard. As we continued, we were joined by several cabs and hansoms, the mysterious conduct of the drivers revealing the mission on which they were employed.'

John Hollingshead, with a longer journey, set out earlier. He had sat up by his fireside rather than go to bed, and now shivered in the night air. A policeman on the beat watched him shut his front door, and it struck Hollingshead that the officer was well aware of his destination. Though a first-class magazine writer, Hollingshead was not a sports writer, and, like Dickens, he knew little of the knuckle game. The cabman who drove him to the station did something to redress his ignorance. The fellow was 'bursting with intelligence of the great prize-fight'.

As the travellers drew near the rail terminus, the flicker of vehicle lamps denoted a convergence of traffic. 'The streets leading directly to London Bridge, and the bridge itself, were noisy with the rattle of wheels,' the *Herald*'s reporter wrote. A wispy mist was rising from the Thames. At the centre of each bridge span, a large gaslight reared torch-like from the balustrade, twinkling on the water and brightening the busy road. The scene the flares illumined was extraordinary. Bleary-eyed and liquor-laden, the Fancy was advancing in varnished coaches and scruffy cabs, packed in coster carts and in vans, by barge and ferry from the north bank, and in hundreds on foot, huddled in scarfs and furs against the chill of the early hours. It seemed, to Henry Miles, a nocturnal version of Derby day.

Outside the station, awaiting its opening, was 'an immense crowd, all desirous of entering. . . . There were dukes, lords, earls and even ministers; there were the first members of the press, merchants, lawyers. . . .' There were butchers from Newgate, fishmongers from Billingsgate, bar-keepers from New York, brokers from Boston; contingents from Bristol, Birmingham, Doncaster; Scots, Welshmen and Irishmen. There were pugilists and poets, civil-servants and publicans, dandies, dips and snatch-artists. 'Several members of the criminal class were apprehended and taken off before the gates opened.' Hansoms, packed to the doors, disgorged all-night revellers, still singing the ditties of the music halls. Uniformed coachmen lugged hampers from Fortnum and Mason. Many excursionists had their breakfasts in their pockets.

The terminus was opened at a quarter to four; the crowd admitted by a number of entrances. 'There were never perhaps so many passengers assembled on a railway platform who knew and addressed each other by their Christian names,' wrote Hollingshead. 'Heavy jaws and high cheekbones were hung out like signboards to mark the members of the fighting trade. . . . Anxious, threatening glances were cast at unknown people, and whispered inquiries passed about who was or was not a plainclothes policeman.' Among many stories circulating, it was said that detectives had been posted on the route from Newmarket with orders to arrest Sayers, who was bound for the station concealed in a horse-box. A persistent rumour had Palmerston spotted among the crowd. According to another, Queen Victoria had demanded immediate news of the fight result.

One train, of thirty carriages, stood in the station. Within minutes, this had filled, and another, of thirty-three carriages, was called up. The South Eastern had a reputation for prompt service. The *Westminster Review*, among other bodies, had acclaimed its operations. But its rolling stock, at the best of times, was not opulent, and the assembly of two mammoth 'specials' stretched its wagon resources. United speciously by the company livery—'an unhealthy flesh tint above and a black line below by way of giving the impression that mortification had set in'—the carriages were of considerable age and assortment. Four-wheel and six-wheel coaches were joined at random with elderly four-wheel vans. Some looked like cottages on wheels; some glorified cattle trucks. 'The styles of the windows included Gothic, Norman and Early English in great variety.' Inside, the partitions were so low that the heads of passengers seated with their backs to them almost collided with the heads of those in the next compartment.

Fight excursionists did not demand luxury. More important to the Fancy was reliable conveyance, and the South Eastern was dependable. Its locomotives, now coupled in tandem to the special trains, regularly knocked up speeds which set their tall stacks juddering; locomen clinging, eyes streaming, to open footplates. Average speeds in excess of forty miles an hour were normal between London and the south coast. The first train was ready to leave London Bridge by four a.m. Among the last to board it was Sayers, appearing fresh and brisk in a 'natty' suit of green twill, having lodged near the terminus overnight.

For a while, fears that Heenan would not arrive—that the police had taken him—were prevalent. Then, some twenty minutes later, he appeared on the platform. Many failed to recognize him. Late-comers were still scrambling for seats on the second train as, walking rapidly between Falkland, Cusick and Macdonald, the American entered a reserved compartment. Moments afterwards, steam gushed to the station roof, couplings clattered, the cars lurched. 'Dawn was just streaking the horizon with grey,' declared a U.S. reporter, 'when the two immense, serpent-like trains set off, we knew not whither.'

Among the passengers that morning was Frederick Locker-Lampson, the English writer. In the last years of his life, Lampson, father of two M.P.s, recalled the excursion as one of his outstanding memories. 'In imagination,' he wrote, 'I am again at the London Bridge terminus with a "there and back" ticket in my pocket. . . . We have taken our seats. There is a considerable delay, but at last a bell rings, there is a snort, and then the monster train glides slowly out of the dimly lighted shed. Once beyond the station, we quicken up. Away we tear in a gale of our own creation—a Faust flight on the devil's mantle.' Creaking and swaying, the trains ploughed through a landscape of countless blackened chimneypots. Most of London had yet to stir.

The man from the *New York Herald* found himself in a compartment with a party of 'very gentlemanly' Londoners. The battle was their single topic of conversation. 'Heenan, they considered, had been outrageously and inhospitably used, in the manner in which he had been hunted from county to county, and they hoped that there would be nothing but a fair fight.' Hollingshead had obtained a seat in the overloaded double compartment of a second-class carriage.

Behind me were a live lord, a live baronet, a member of parliament, the very gentlemanly editor of a distinguished sporting paper [*Dowling*], an aristocratic Scotsman, a clergyman of the Church of England, and a renowned poet of the tender passions [*possibly Coventry Patmore*]. . . . By the side of me was a young, cheerful, round-faced Australian settler who had travelled 15,000 miles to see the fight and transact "a little other business of minor importance". He looked the sort of man to go round the world with a cigar in his mouth and his hands in his pockets. Opposite was a mild, blinking gentleman of Jewish aspect who talked fluently and seemed to know all the minor deities of the ring. By his side was a drowsy, ragged pugilist [*Jack Grant*] whose scalp had been taken by Sayers eight years earlier. Most passengers were sleepy, having been up all night, and conversation rested chiefly with the Australian and the Jew.

Before the city was fully behind them, dawn had broken. Peering through a smutty window, Henry Miles perceived 'that peculiar tint which foretold brilliant sunny weather'. It was not the only thing that Miles saw. Beside the track stood officers of the law in countless numbers, 'all armed with cutlasses'. Apprehension seized the travellers. 'Looking out, we found the road on both sides lined with London policemen,' averred an American. 'Every fifteen or twenty feet for more than a mile was a policeman, and occasionally we passed a little knot of three or four, with a mounted man at their head, who, upon our approach, galloped off as if to communicate with other parties. This looked ominous. Our party in the car began to express supreme disgust at the prospect of interference.'

Soon, it became evident that the trains were not to be pulled up. Mayne's constabulary, deployed in the more open parts of the metropolis, was there to prevent the Fancy stopping. The passengers relaxed again. Some gestured lewdly at 'the crushers'. The locos sped on, emitting sparks and thick smoke. Derisive howls reached the 'blues' on the slip-stream. At length, the Fancy settled to rest once more. The chat in Hollingshead's compartment was desultory.

'"Saw a good fight in Melbourne about a week afore I left," said the Aussie.

"Did you?" said the Jew.

"There's a fortune there for any man about eight stun nine."

The pug slowly opened one eye.

"There's no good man there under nine stun," said the Aussie.

The Jew suggested a name.

"Used up," declared the Aussie.

"Joss Humphrey?"

"Bouncy. Wants it taken out of him. Fights at ten stun: gives a stun but won't strip for less than a pot o' gold."

"*What* name?" The pug opened both eyes inquiringly.

"Joss Humphrey."

"Oh . . ." The pug went to sleep again.'

The trains steamed on, now through dewy rustic scenes, still following the main Dover and Brighton line which channelled traffic south from London. Anticipating trouble, the local authorities were watching out. On small country stations—simple staggered platforms with single-storey clapboard offices—solitary policemen watched, blue-nosed, as the excursion passed. 'Official scarecrows,' Hollingshead called them. Others shivered under trees, while a detachment of mounted officers cantered on a coach-road beside the rails. At Reigate junction, in Surrey, there was a burst of excitement as those familiar with railway geography noted a change of track. The trains had switched from the main southbound lines and were running west towards Hampshire. The diversion confounded the constabulary, for Betchworth, Dorking and Gomshall passed without sign of a policeman. The 'blues' were waiting vainly at points towards Brighton. The outlook, wrote Miles, was of peace and serenity. 'Scarcely a soul was to be seen beyond husbandmen proceeding to their daily avocations.'

Not far from the timbered market-town of Guildford, the locomotives stopped to take on water. Shalford junction was close ahead, and here they turned southwest on a line which crossed the Surrey–Hampshire heathlands. 'In a short time,' Miles reported, 'we entered the wild district where the military camp of Aldershot is situated, the deserted appearance satisfying all that those to whom the selection of the *locale* had been entrusted had made a happy choice.' The full orb of the sun had risen above spinney and hedgerow. Gorse and heather grew beside the track. Careering past the hamlet of Witley, the crowded 'specials' plunged into the wilderness approaching Farnborough.

'It was near seven o'clock when the first train discharged its burthen in the station, after a most pleasant journey through rural England, which, illumined by glorious sun and shooting forth in vernal beauty, must have inspired all with gratification, not least the Americans,' exclaimed Miles. In fact, the length of the trains far exceeded that of the station platform, and the bulk of the Fancy descended directly to the grassy banks. For many, a release from the city was exhilarating. Locker-Lampson treasured the moment. 'For several months I had been confined to London pavement and the dead wood of the office desk. How well I remember the strange delightfulness of the green trees, the fresh grass cool beneath my feet, and the gracious April air as it played upon my face! A lark was soaring and singing far above our heads, rejoicing in his glorious privacy; clerks and costermongers were clambering fences and leaping dykes.'

Already Oliver, the ring-maker, was heading across country with his commissariat. Like boys out of school, the travellers, in their tens of hundreds, gave lusty chase. It was a sight such as even Miles had not seen before. Coat tails and scarves flying, clutching top hats and bowlers, old and young, lords and commoners, away they dashed with the gusto of harriers. There was about half a mile to cover, in places marshy, with several obstacles.

Well up in the charge were Bob Fuller, the athlete, tiny Jimmy Holden, showing remarkable agility for his stature, and Harry Hill of New York's Exchange saloon. Several score Americans advanced with whoops and war cries. Englishmen had probably not seen such a demonstration of transatlantic exuberance in the mass since Chippewa and Lundy's Lane. Morrissey and Cunningham, the Tipton Slasher, a score of burly bruisers, were there in the leading pack. Behind came the Birdman, scanning the hedges for early nests, lads in their teens and stowaway mongrel dogs from the East End on the outing of a lifetime. In the rear, among elderly gentlemen with *pince-nez* and overweight plutocrats, was an enthusiast of such advanced age and frailty that he had to be supported by two hired pugs. A British journalist picked up the story at the first jump:

Ahead went the ring-maker, who cleared a wide ditch and hedge; and after him came the crowd. Such mishaps we never remember to have witnessed! Not one half of the crowd who attempted to leap the hedge and ditch succeeded, but either slipped backwards when they reached the opposite bank, or fell headlong in the stream. In one place, there were two frail spars or rails across, and here several adventurous individuals tried to cross. Some succeeded, until a young sprig of the aristocracy, accompanied by his groom, broke the bridge in the middle and dropped decorously into the stagnant water. A dozen of the humbler class of excursionists coined money by ferrying fellow travellers on their backs.

Fuller slung Jimmy Holden jockey-fashion on his shoulders and leaped the ditch. The Birdman, rolling his trousers over bony legs, waded heron-like in the mire. The field pounded on behind its leaders. 'There was a continuation of mishaps. Clothes were torn, shoes stuck in bogs, men fell into stinging nettles. The Americans suffered most from the last cause. Evidently unfamiliar with a plant indigenous to our soil, they rushed through the nettle banks, emerging sadly smarting from their exploits.' Closely followed by his son, Fred, the veteran commissary led the charge at a cracking pace. Estimates of the numbers involved varied widely, but the occupants of sixty-three railway carriages would hugely have outnumbered Farnborough's population, and there were many others. Tipped off beforehand, some had made their own travel arrangements to reduce expenses. Parties of sporting men from the adjoining countryside had joined the onrush. Off-duty soldiers turned up from Aldershot, where thirty thousand troops were stationed. Not only army but naval officers were present. Many others, including merchants, horse-dealers, contractors and doctors, had materialized by unexplained means. Seeming to swell by the minute, the Fancy poured to the appointed spot. News of its arrival hit the village like a thunderbolt.

20 The Magnesia Boy

This said—the Heroes for the fight prepare,
Brace their big Limbs and brawny Bodies Bare.
The sturdy Sinews all aghast behold,
And ample Shoulders of Atlean Mould
PAUL WHITEHEAD

At the first garbled account of the invasion, the people of Farnborough bolted indoors, leaving the local representative of the law to investigate. Nervously, the constable, a part-timer, set out for the station. Almost immediately, the hubbub of the crowd became audible, and, looking towards the screening birches, he paused in astonishment. The trees were smothered with dark shapes, as if a flock of gigantic rooks had pitched in them. The shapes were human: agile members of the Fancy who had found a natural gallery near the ring. Closer to the station, the sight of the two trains confirmed the constable's worst fears. The station master was less than co-operative. Asked to transmit a police message by telegraph, he resorted to the standard delaying tactics of the South Eastern. Red-faced, the constable redirected his steps towards the South Western company's station.

Farnborough had already adopted a state of siege. According to Hollingshead, farmers had barricaded their dwellings when the trains appeared. Cottage doors were barred; the village shop secured against entry; watch-dogs strained threateningly on their chains. Fearfully, the populace awaited the deluge. When it became clear that the enemy had halted, a few villagers ventured from their homes to scout. Soon, a trickle of curious neighbours reached the meadows, cautiously join-ing the fight crowd. Maybe the bald Goodfellow, Watts the tippler, resilient Nat Attfield, were among them. The sporting chroniclers could not tell. Hollingshead identified the locals simply as a smattering of 'labourers, village women and children, and a country idiot with limp arms and gaping mouth—the only truly innocent spectator at the fight'.

In their wildest dreams they could not have conjured the pageant of the championship. 'By a quarter past seven o'clock,' wrote an American, 'the ropes were stretched and everything in readiness. The ground was soft and damp, and felt as if it might be easy to fall upon. The ring-keepers, twenty-one of the principal London pugilists, were stationed on the outside of the ropes to keep order. The crowd waited impatiently.' Inner-ring tickets, purchased at ten shillings each, entitled their holders to sit in front of the main concourse, either on the damp ground or on seats hired from a small-time London *entrepreneur*, Billy Duncan. Prominent at the ringside were friends and backers of the contestants: for Sayers, Gideon, Fuller, Morrissey, Cunningham; for Heenan, Falkland, Charley Lynch (American lightweight champion) and, among others, the 'Boy's' uncle, a man named Moore.

In Heenan's corner, the burly Macdonald wore braces over shirt-sleeves and sported a pill-box hat. Cusick, in bow-tie and 'bum-freezer', shuffled anxiously. Sayers's seconds wore rink-smocks. Brunton was bare-headed; the angular Welsh in a peaked sea cap. Large square baskets containing bottles and sponges stood at the stake posts. The strength of the press corps was unprecedented in ring history. Apart from leading British 'dailies', periodicals and miscellanies, American journals were well represented—a novel feature at an English ring. There was even a reporter from France, where prize-fighting was unknown. On the ground, near the American corner, sat George Wilkes, notebook in hand. The familiar figure of Henry Miles was much in evidence. So was that of Dowling, elected now as referee.

Three or four illustrators were present, including Thomas Nash, and sketched busily by the ropes. The *New York Illustrated News* had sent an engraver, A. V. S. Anthony, to England to collect Nash's pictures and prepare blocks on the *Vanderbilt* as she steamed home. The *London Illustrated News* had promised readers portraits of the fighters and action pictures in its first issue after the contest.

Following its hectic cross-country gambol, the Fancy was 'orderly and quiet, all on tip-toe, anxious to see the start of an affair which, for the past three months, had been the subject of so much talk and anxiety'. The tree-climbers had settled in their perches. Ginger beer and orange pedlars, having travelled from London with their merchandise, were doing business; 'fine wirers' prospecting victims. Eighteen Americans were among those who later declared the loss of gold watches at the fight. Betting was moderate at 7 to 4 on Sayers. 'Most of the punters seemed to have already placed money,' commented a spectator, 'and were content to wait the next developments.'

At about twenty past seven, Sayers appeared at the ringside, flipped his hat across the ropes and ducked after it. The cheering was tumultuous. 'Sayers's face was a deep sallow brown, like a square block of walnut wood. He was slightly nervous on facing the company.' Almost immediately, Heenan, wearing an overcoat over a grey suit, stepped into the ring, and the fighters saw each other for the first time. For a moment, they exchanged appraising glances, then advanced to shake hands amid more applause. According to Harry Hill, who was near by, 'Sayers walked across to Heenan, who kind of met him halfway. Sayers says, "How are you, my boy? A fine morning, this." "Yes," says Heenan, "we've got a beautiful morning for it." "Yes," says Sayers, "if a man can't fight such a day as this, he can't fight at all."'

Formalities took some minutes. Seconds and officials were introduced; colours attached to the stakes. The toss for corners, giving Heenan the advantage, caused a general shuffle as he chose to put the sun behind his back. To Hollingshead, a newcomer at such affairs, it seemed that 'everything was conducted to superstitiously observed rules. There were almost as many ceremonies as at a Coronation'.

Swiftly, the contestants shed their outer garments. Beneath them, they wore white fighting breeches and stockings, with high quartered boxing shoes. Heenan's aroused comment, being elastic sided rather than of the normal lace-up variety. 'When stripped,' observed an American correspondent, 'Sayers showed a splendid development of chest and neck, and apparently more breadth of shoulder than his opponent, but Heenan towered over him.' Locker-Lampson recalled the murmur of admiration from the crowd as Heenan's physique became evident. 'He was at once recognized as the most magnificent athlete ever seen in the prize-ring.' The American had shaved off his moustache and had his hair cut close in the traditional fighting style.

He looked extremely fit and handsome. Bob Brettle, beside Lampson, expressed the thought in both minds: 'Well, Tom may beat him, but I'm beggared if he'll eat him!'

At eleven stone, Sayers weighed some twenty pounds lighter than had Morrissey at Long Point. Heenan was thirteen stone eight pounds. 'Tom's work seemed indeed cut out,' admitted Miles. 'Heenan stood fully four inches over him, with the longer reach. Every muscle on the American's broad back, shoulders and arms was well developed, and evidenced enormous power. His legs were rather light, but not lacking wire and activity. His skin was exceedingly fair and transparent, and shone like that of a thoroughbred.' Quick to note his lack of colour, a cockney in the crowd announced cheerfully: 'It's the Magnesia Boy!'

Of Sayers, Henry Miles wrote: 'Tom looked brown and hard as nails: his well-knit frame seemed fitter than we have seen it for years. He appeared visibly older even than when he fought Brettle, but, considering what he has gone through, this is not to be wondered at. The only points in which there seemed any advantage on his side were in his loins and legs, which were cast in a decidedly stronger mould than those of his tall opponent. . . . That Tom had the remotest qualms as to the result we do not for an instant believe. He smiled confidently.'

Heenan also contrived to look composed, though, to Hollingshead, the equanimity of both men appeared strained. 'There was a false laugh on each face which was meant to be agreeable.' If Sayers had cause to fear his adversary's size and relative youthfulness, the 'Boy' had equal cause for apprehension. Sayers's toughness and fighting talents were on record. That his own were not was attested by the market. The Fancy had tagged the match several ways: weight against science, vigour against tenacity, all-round athleticism against special skill, New World enthusiasm against Old World phlegm. None was entirely apt; each appealed in certain quarters. Alleged national endowments were boasted by both sides. Locker-Lampson recollected a strange tremor as the men took their positions. 'There was something in this great fight which the whole nation recognized. . . . It affected all classes. . . . It was magnetic.'

The green square glistened with fierce promises. To romantics, heady with spring air and sunshine, the scene was set on the field of the Cloth of Gold; to punters, the turf was a money mart. To Morrissey, squatting by the ropes, settlement seemed imminent on old debts. To patriots, trumpets heralded native truths. To Miles, the shades of Entellus and Dares hovered overhead. Others slavered for blood and guts. The pugs themselves eyed each other with private thoughts. Perhaps they shared the consolation of irony—neither could suffer greater ignominy at a man's hands than had already been dealt him by a woman's. At least they knew the rules of this battle.

At a minute to half-past seven, a roar of applause greeted the advance of the fighters to scratch. As they paused, arms poised for a signal, the roar died. Gideon fingered his watch-chain. Lampson tingled. 'The atmosphere is suddenly breathless with tension, hushed with an eerie silence. Trees seemed to cease their rustling. The twitter of birds breaks off in mid-air. It is a stark silence which spreads quietly across England, across the deep Atlantic, to wash against the shores of America. The two men stand motionless, big with battle.' The crowd, too, was motionless. Hollingshead felt uncomfortable. Heenan flexed his shoulders. The hard, sad face of Sayers became intent. There was a shout:

'Time!'

21 An Eye for an Arm

Each felt his balance trim and true—
Each up to square his mauleys threw—
Each tried his best to draw his man—
The feint, the dodge, the opening plan . . .
. . . Again each iron mauley swung,
And loud the counter-hitting rung
                    W. M. THACKERAY (attrib.)

The battle of the champions opened at a tempo characteristic of the prize-ring. For what would have been well over a round under Queensberry boxing rules, the combatants performed a flat-footed ritual skirmish, as innocuous as it was ponderous. Fists and arms wove menacing patterns, heads bobbed and inclined, bodies swayed with unhurried elegance. Among uninitiated spectators such as Hollingshead, the preliminaries evoked cynicism. 'For nearly five minutes,' complained one, 'neither pugilist gave or received a blow.' More appreciative of an occasion of unique importance, the Fancy voiced encouragement. The pugilists responded with some play for the audience. Sayers, evading a lead from Heenan, shrugged ironically, the melancholy clown. Heenan shook his head and grinned when Sayers missed.

The sparring drifted toward Heenan's corner, where a praetorian guard of some fifty or sixty Americans had massed to protect their man's interests. The sun, still low, made Sayers blink and squint. Suddenly, the temper changed. Heenan's face twisted as a brown fist caught his nose. Counters followed. Sayers found the face again, ducking his opponent's blow. A dark effluence seeped from Heenan's nostrils. The prelude was over. It had happened in an instant—the instant which transformed every fight crowd. There was, said Hollingshead, uproarious applause as Sayers drew first blood.

'Unruly spectators leaped up from the grass and danced wildly near the ropes, while the ring-keepers applied their sticks without stint or favour to heads and shoulders. . . . Large sums of money were offered by rough and shabby-looking people on either fighter. Aristocratic eyes stared intensely through eye-glasses.'

Heenan restored the balance shortly afterwards. Closing to wrestle, he caught Sayers round the neck with a powerful arm, and, as the Englishman replied with half-arm punches, threw him with convincing ease. The first round had been a warm-up. Appetizers had been dispensed on both sides, without much effect on the market. Fifty pounds to twenty on Sayers found no takers. The British champion advanced purposefully for the second round, deflecting and eluding Heenan's lunges with the dexterity that had baffled big men for many years. Again, the brown fist shot into Heenan's face. Smarting, the American lashed back. His supporters roared as he caught Sayers on the forehead, and, closing, flung him violently to the ground. The 'Boy' landed with his full weight on Sayers's ribs.

If the winded champion was conscious of the cheers from Heenan's corner, they must have been capped by Brunton's urgency: 'Don't let him wrestle you, Tom! You can't wrestle him!'

Sayers came out warily, backing off as the 'Boy' advanced. Heenan's speed, for his size, was unsettling. So was the force behind his left hand. Striking the bridge of Sayers's nose, it sent him sprawling. Spectators gasped. There was no mistaking the Englishman's puzzled frown as he faced the fourth round. The incredible was happening. Heenan went straight to him, brushed off a warning shot, and put him down with another left. This time, it found the jaw. Sayers was carried to his corner, as Hollingshead put it, 'like a Guy Fawkes'. His supporters were thunderstruck. No one had treated the champion this way. Was it possible that the vanquisher of Poulson, Paddock and Perry had met his match—that the hard man of Camden was sinking so easily?

Round five. Sayers's face flushed. He tried to evade his man. Heenan threw a wild punch, took a counter on the nose, then promptly dropped the Englishman. It was a massive blow. Turning to his seconds, he 'threw up both arms in jubilation'. According to a British reporter, his supporters were 'jumping in the air like antelopes, waving hats and shouting as though mad'. Those close to him thumped his back 'as if desirous of testing the thickness of The Boy's hide'. Others chanted 'Five to one on Heenan!'—odds unsupported by the betting, but sufficiently indicative of the mood. Among the bruisers struggling to control the throng, Jerry Noon grunted dismally. 'It's all up with Tom,' he said. Minutes later, and Sayers on his back again, the assertion seemed difficult to gainsay. Despondency was widespread. As the *Saturday Review* observed afterwards: 'The majority of spectators beheld a sight very different from that for which they had bargained. It was not to see the Champion of England repeatedly knocked clean off his legs that so many Englishmen had travelled to Farnborough.'

The fighters presented contrasting images. Heenan was visibly excited, perhaps over-confident. His delighted gestures at each knock-down expressed not only natural exuberance but the unexpectedness of developments. It is doubtful if victory seemed far away to him. At the same time, he had received enough blows from Sayers to be less euphoric than his wilder supporters. Those punches, deriving effect from skilful timing, were more dangerous than they looked. Heenan's neck and face bore revealing marks. Sayers glowered lugubriously. None was better placed to judge events up to that point. He had taken the falls; he possessed the experience. If one thing must have been clear in his professional mind, it was that Heenan, gambling the safety of his hands on a decisive blow, was taking a bold risk.

The Camden bruiser was resilient. He had yet to get the hang of the American, but there was time for that. No man, however strong, had ever stopped him with a knock-down. More worrying to Sayers, though less evident to the crowd, was the sensation in his right arm: the throbbing pain that had followed its use to deflect a blow in the sixth round. If the arm got worse, his position might indeed become desperate. Meanwhile, he summoned up all his ring-generalship. He came out for the seventh round grim-faced.

The later drama and sensational climax of the great fight were founded in its seventh and eighth rounds, as ruggedly daunting as they were long. Of thirteen and twenty minutes respectively, they held the Fancy in high suspense. 'A constant roar of voices was raised round the ring,' recounted Hollingshead. 'People at the back made frantic attempts to mount the shoulders of those in front. Nervous betting men, with heavy stakes on the outcome, got out of the mêlée and walked about the meadow. The wind hissed through the trees, and the hundreds who clung to the bending branches shouted wildly for their favourites.' So ferocious were the exchanges as Sayers fought to restore his dented fortune that unseasoned reporters were sickened.

'I cannot give our readers a technical description,' admitted the representative of a New York journal, 'it is the first prize-fight I ever witnessed—and most certainly it will be the last.' Even Frederick Locker-Lampson, whose praise for the fighters was unreserved, recalled their injuries as 'hideous and loathsome'.

Heenan pursued his head start with eagerness. Shoulders working, arms swinging, he pitched into his adversary. Macdonald had counselled him to take his time. Instead, he attacked over-anxiously, missing with both hands. Sayers evaded several sallies. At last, he was adjusting to Heenan's pace, beginning to anticipate the 'Boy's' moves. Sayers looked more like a champion. The American charged again. This time, Sayers braced himself and countered with a shot to the right cheek. It staggered Heenan, rasping flesh from his cheek-bone. He was barely collected when Sayers found the same spot, compounding the gash and the swelling. Heenan went to his corner to sponge his face. Both seconds now censured his impatience. 'Cusick told him to steady up, not to rush his fences, and the Boy seemed to acquiesce.'

Sayers stood in the centre of the ring, right arm throbbing. The limb had stiffened. He held it awkwardly across his chest. Heenan returned to him more cautiously, fell short with two lefts, then missed with an upper-cut. The target was no longer where he reckoned it. In place of the convenient victim of the early rounds flitted the will-o'-the-wisp who had reduced Paddock and Perry to enraged despair; a fighting shadow with a hatchet fist. Relentlessly, as Heenan strove to put his man down, the hatchet chopped at his mangled cheek. It was the turn of the American to look confused, and of the London fans to get back at his supporters. 'Two to one on Sayers!' they chanted delightedly.

Harry Hill had no liking for cockney wit. The Londoners behaved, he said, 'damned shamefully. Every time Sayers got a little the upper hand, they'd sing out, "'Ere's another sure fing, ain't it, ho, ho, ho; take 'im away," and suchlike expressions, blackguarding Heenan and his friends in the worst style.'

Half-way through the seventh, Sayers raised his sights from Heenan's cheek to his right eye. It stopped a brutal blow, closing as he groped for a cold sponge. Impudently, Sayers idled nearby while Cusick swabbed his fighter, examining the outcome of his handiwork. Heenan's good eye glinted. Brushing the sponge aside, he strode forward angrily, throwing his powerful left with savage force. Sayers took it on his crippled arm. Wincing, he swayed from a second shot. It landed with enough impact to unbalance him and conclude the round. There was no doubt about Sayers's satisfaction. Rolling on the turf, he kicked his legs up in a smart salute.

The British crowd was back in humour. As the seconds worked on the fighters, Sayers was the more composed. 'Heenan exhibited a little nervousness,' declared the *Herald*. 'Sayers's countenance was unchanged.' Gideon passed him a flask through the ropes, and he sucked at it. ' "I done him that time," said Tom. "It's an eye for an arm now." "You can't pretend that's a fair exchange," Johnnie said. "You can if I do the other eye," replied Tom. Harry was rubbing embrocation on the swollen limb.' Round eight was a grisly slog. Sayers opened the American's mauled cheek, chiselling constantly at the head. Heenan's left flew dangerously, mashing his adversary's lips and gums. Old hands of the boxing press scribbled their jaunty prose:

Tom crept in and pop went his left on the plague spot . . . once more on the cheek with a slogger. Heenan retaliated sharply on the snout, but was stopped in a second attempt when Tom nailed him heavily and got away. Persevering, the Boy left a bump on the gallant Tom. More sparring until a severe counter-exchange took place, in which Tom got a hot 'un on the whistler which shook his ivories and turned the tap on. It was a staggerer, but Tom recovered and went to his man, Heenan getting another rum one on the cheek and dropping his left on Tom's sneezer. Both now indulged in a wipe and washed their mouths out. They came again, like giants refreshed . . .

Hollingshead's was a different view:

With the sun full on it, Sayer's face was like a battered copper tea-kettle. He was frequently spitting blood. His right arm was stiff and helpless. Heenan's right eye was closed with a huge lump of blue flesh; his upper lip puffed out as if there were six rows of gums and teeth behind it. When Sayers gave a telling hit, he looked inquisitively at Heenan to see what he had done to him. When Heenan knocked Sayers down, he turned and opened his swollen mouth in gasping satisfaction. . . . A few oaths were heard, but not many. Faces round the inner circle became paler, lips more compressed. Outsiders leaped up and down ceaselessly to glimpse the ring. The smacking blows resounded, and their effect was described mouth to mouth for excited inquirers.

The voices of Morrissey and others, bawling advice to Sayers, drowned in the clamour. Charlie Lynch was fighting an invisible adversary in his mimed encouragements to Heenan. The Englishman's right arm, perceptibly thickening, had become little more than a bruised shield. Sayers threw it, once, at Heenan's left eye. It reached the target, but too feebly to do any damage. Mostly, it was the hatchet left against Heenan's double-handed thrusts. Toe to toe, they contested the last minutes of round eight with fearful blows. Harry Hill watched with awed admiration. 'Jack Heenan took every hit in first rate humour,' he said later. 'He tried to laugh two or three times after Sayers had cut him, but his face was so out of shape you couldn't tell if he was laughing or crying.' Hill believed his compatriot would have been in worse shape if his second had not checked his pace, and constantly counselled him. 'If he'd gone on his own hook I don't think he'd got along too well.' Sayers was even tougher than the New Yorker had expected. 'The more knocks he took, the better he seemed to fight. It didn't appear to produce much effect on him, for he'd fall with the blows and throw his legs up as if it was all sport. Damnedest sort of sport I ever seen.'

There was nothing sportive about the shot that closed the eighth round. It connected cleanly with Sayers's jaw and put him down in a limp heap. After two mammoth bouts, he badly needed a respite, a spell in which to 'nurse his years' as *Bell's Life* put it. Formidably, the younger man showed no debility. In a remarkable demonstration of athletic energy, he harried Sayers remorselessly in the ninth round, advancing with even greater vigour in the tenth. Silenced by its astonishment, the crowd watched the American rush forward, pluck his adversary off his feet, and hurl him to the turf with apparent ease. The hush was broken by an ironical voice with a transatlantic accent: 'Well, Sayers, are you staying for another round?'

At this stage, attention was diverted momentarily from the arena to the fringe of the audience. During the ninth round, two police officers had appeared, joined now by a couple more. With little compunction about embarrassing its rival, the South Western Railway had employed its communications at the behest of the constabulary. From county headquarters at Winchester, orders were passing via telegraph and messengers for the convergence of as strong a force as practicable upon Farnborough. Winchester itself, thirty miles from the battle (forty by rail), was unlikely to get men to the scene in time. But detachments of the Hampshire constabulary were much nearer.

Among other towns and villages, Basingstoke (about fifteen miles from Farnborough), Hook and Winchfield (less than ten miles), and Fleet and Aldershot (three miles), were handy to law officers and served by the South Western. Aldershot maintained a police establishment to handle problems arising from the soldiery. Within an hour of the fight commencing, blue uniforms were crossing Laffan's Plain, the bleak stretch south of Farnborough. Heading north from the shanties which had mushroomed in the region of the army camp, they traversed the canal known locally as 'Barge River', skirted the evergreens and palings of a large estate, and heard the distant roar of the fight crowd.

Meanwhile, the first brace of officers to reinforce Farnborough's constable had arrived from the more immediate surrounds, summoned from hamlet and village by anxious farmers. Neither the solid mass of humanity in the meadow nor its unwelcoming attitude encouraged intervention. Prudently, the small group of rustic 'blues' stuck its thumbs in its belts and awaited support from the converging squads.

22 The Mill Continues

Two hours and more the fight had sped,
Near unto ten it drew,
But still opposed one-armed to blind,
They stood those dauntless two . . .
W. M. THACKERAY (attrib.)

At 7.45 a.m., the loco attendant who had stayed with the first train to keep the fire stoked watched a party of constables clamber over a hedge towards the fight crowd. His mate, and the railway guards, had joined the Fancy at the ringside. The clamour of the spectators surged across the meadows in crescendo. In his knapsack was half a loaf, a chunk of cheese and a pint of tea in a beer bottle, swathed in an old sock to keep it hot. Climbing down from the footplate, he sat on the grass bank to picnic.

Amid the shoving, vociferous concourse, the correspondent of the *Journal des Débats* formulated the rough theme of his report:

This struggle brought face to face the Old World and the New— Old England and Young America. The American giant is tall and strong, like the trees of the New World. His frame is in proportion to the forests, the lakes, the rivers of America. He reminds us of primeval strength, and of the men who measured seven cubits in height, as in the early ages of the world. Face to face with him we have the Old World, the product of the ages that have passed: the highest product of civilization, the creature of art. And yet, after all, these two athletes are of the same blood, sprung from the same stock.

It is England in its youth and England in its manhood, but the race is the same. . . . What are the attributes of the English race?

What but endurance, patience and energy, often latent but always fierce, and which never knows defeat—an obstinacy that will not be conquered, and a secret oath to die rather than yield. In the story of this fight we find one and all these attributes.

Obstinacy was true enough. Between the tenth and twentieth rounds, both fighters were slower to scratch, less hurried in rising from the second's knee, but the bouts retained their viciousness. Repeatedly, Sayers was put down. Stubbornly, he came back. Occasionally, Heenan dropped with him. Two or three times, the Englishman fell as a saving ploy. More often, he was knocked off his feet by the larger man. Heenan no longer signalled exuberance. In the thirteenth, he turned to Falkland after dropping his man and croaked: 'That's one for you, Fred!' But he could barely force the words from his twisted mouth. Round fifteen: Sayers in a heap from a right to the jaw. Round sixteen: Sayers down from a blow in the mouth. Round nineteen: Sayers thrown and fallen on by Heenan.

Triumphant cheering from Heenan's supporters greeted these events. But the American was paying dearly, not only in the currency of Sayers's effective arm but with the pain from his own swollen knuckles. His face registered the cost when he landed a heavy shot. The durability of the Englishman's lentous features was remarkable. Though bloody, his countenance scarcely matched its punishment. 'Heenan's mug was decidedly the most disfigured,' affirmed *Bell's Life*. An American correspondent made the same point:

> Sayers did not show as much punishment, although he had received some terrific blows on the head . . . both men, bruised and bloody, fought on bravely—if such things can be called so—and well they were supported and encouraged by the cheering. . . . Two masses of muscle, directed by two brains, performed the work allotted to them. We never could have believed that anything human could sustain such continued punishing; but a little water, a little brandy, a little rubbing, a few words of consolation, seemed to keep the machines in motion.

Eight-thirty. Round twenty-one, and into the second hour of fighting. Constant cheers and counter-cheers. A squad of perspiring police, arriving after a forced march, glimpsed two battered figures 'locked like jungle trees' at the centre of the bellowing, gesticulating mob of spectators. It was clear, according to a British sport journalist, that the greatest championship ever fought was in progress. 'The gluttony and bottom of Tom Sayers are too proverbial to need comment; but as rumours had been flying that Heenan was destitute of these qualities, we deem it right to proclaim that a gamer, more determined fellow never pulled off a shirt.' Observed *The Times*:

> The scene had become one of the most intense and brutal excitement. There were shouts to Heenan to keep his antagonist in the sun, to close with him and smash him, while the friends of Sayers called to him to take his time as the American's sight was diminishing. The bets were even on both men. [*Actually, offers of 5 to 4 on Heenan now prevailed, but most punters were too engrossed in the action to place bets.*] When Sayers was knocked almost senseless under a tremendous blow, there were cheers from the Americans till the fields echoed. . . . At this time, the police who had come on the scene did their best to reach the ring, but the crowd kept them back.

About a dozen constables had tried to force a path through the mob with slight effect save for the loss of tempers and the odd helmet. While the police withdrew to regroup and await fresh reinforcements to their increasing numbers, Cusick reached through the ropes and grabbed a stool for his fighter. Immediate protests from the opposite corner prompted referee Dowling to order its removal as contrary to the rules. Heenan kicked the offending object from the ring and charged at Sayers. Making to retreat, the Englishman turned suddenly and swung at Heenan with his damaged arm. It came up feebly, only to drop to his side, limp. Crashing forward, the American bowled his foe over and dropped on him. It seemed to those watching that the 'Boy's' energy was limitless.

Sayers came out slowly for the next round, looking exhausted. For a moment, he surveyed the powerful frame of the enemy as if pondering the extent of the crisis. His friends were silent—Fuller, taut with apprehension; Brunton, florid and sweating; Gideon, grim faced; the diminutive Holden, peering anxiously under the arm-pits of the ring-keepers. If the English champion needed reminding of the tactics that had once enabled just such a weary bruiser, Nat Langham, to snatch victory against the odds, it came anonymously from the crowd. 'Put up his shutters, Tom!' called a hoarse voice. 'The eye, Tom—shut up the other eye!' He shuffled away from his adversary, twisting, dodging hoping to regain strength.

Round twenty-four: Sayers down again, ominously to a slight knock. Round twenty-five: Heenan bores in and throws the Englishman. 'Tom looks all-in, rubbery with fatigue.' Then, abruptly in the twenty-sixth, the brown fist found its objective, fully on the 'Boy's' eye. Heenan stiffened. Furiously, he lashed back, staggering Sayers. The Camden bruiser shook his head. Encouraged by his bull's-eye, he returned to the target. The wounded fighters stood square-on, exchanging blows. Frantically, the sporting journalists scribbled: 'Heenan on the tato-trap . . . Tom on the nose, a smasher that draws the cork . . . Heenan on the snorer, rocking the weary Tom. . . .' The end of another round. Sayers was on his knees. Overcome by excitement, Heenan struck him while he was down. Dowling dismissed the foul as accidental.

In the next bout, to the delight of the British crowd, Sayers put another shot on Heenan's working eye, which began to close. English optimism was premature. The American immediately ran his man to the ropes and forced him down. Three more rounds saw Sayers desperately evading the 'Boy's' tireless onslaughts. The Englishman's limbs were too leaden to succeed for long. Heenan rushed him, pummelled him, threw him, and crushed him with sheer weight. By the twenty-ninth, one or two voices were calling for Sayers to be stopped for his own sake. Defiantly, he pushed out his sound arm and carried on. Only the spongy swelling round Heenan's knuckles saved his foe from extinction. But the American, too, was in trouble. Increasingly wild charges indicated his predicament. His vision was failing. 'Both eyes appeared to have been stung by a swarm of bees.'

Said Harry Hill of Heenan's injuries: 'I never saw such a head on a man in my life, and I never want to again. It was horrible, bloody, bruised and swelled out of shape.' Reported *Bell's Life*: 'Heenan's remaining eye was quickly closing and evidently he had no time to lose. He was the stronger on his legs, but his punishment was far more visible than Tom's. He rushed at Tom in the thirtieth round, literally running over him.' Consultations ensued tensely in the corners. Brunton was urging Sayers to evade his man, to keep to the blind side, to hang on at all costs. Cusick was telling Heenan to throw everything at Sayers before the American's left eye became as sightless as the right. The crowd was breathless; excited to 'a pitch hardly equalled in pugilistic history'.

Behind it, preparations were taking place for another battle. By now, the police were mustered in substantial force. Led by a beefy Hampshire sergeant with a moustache 'as red and bushy as a stoat's tail', a score or so constables advanced resolutely on the rear of the concourse in phalanx, intent on reaching the ring itself. Oblivious of this diversion, the pugilists trundled to scratch again. Sayers swayed and raised his left in slow motion, a parody of weariness. Heenan cocked his head like a sick hen. Peering as if through a thickening meadow-mist, he barged forward swinging his raw fists. They missed hopelessly. He peered again, threw his left, and connected. Sayers was picked up by his seconds and returned for more. Another wild one on the cheek put him down again. Now, Heenan came to scratch in a blind rush. The two collided and fell in a tangled heap. It was nine-thirty. They had fought for two hours.

The police had fought a matter of minutes, but already faces in their ranks were bleeding and tunics ripped. Grimly, they swung their sticks at the resisting crowd. As those in their path pressed forward to avoid the charge, others nearer the ring were impelled towards the stakes and ropes. Vainly, the ring-keepers struggled to hold them back. The fight proper entered round thirty-six. Heenan, out in a stumbling, groping sortie, grabbed Sayers by the neck and tried to crush him. Unable to distinguish more than the shadow of his stubborn foe, the American had abandoned hope of a knock-down win and settled to wrestle a submission from his adversary. Sayers slipped through his arms to the scarred turf.

The Englishman could barely make scratch for another bout. Summoning the dregs of his energy, he watched Heenan raise himself from Macdonald's knee and flounder towards him like a drunken giant. Sayers braced his legs and let his fist fly. Twice it smashed into the slit which remained of Heenan's left eye. Blindly, the 'Boy' reeled forward with stretched arms, as if reaching for some dimly perceived ghost. Simultaneously, the crowd, recoiling from the battling constables, overran the ring-keepers and surged into the arena.

Discovering Sayers with his hands, Heenan applied a neck-hold, forcing his opponent's throat against the ropes. The scene now was of wholesale confusion. Policemen were fighting spectators at the ring-side. Supporters were in the ring. Referee Dowling, submerged in the scrimmage, lost view of the pugilists, as did some reporters. Amid a bedlam of voices and insidious darkness, Heenan was conscious only of the need to maintain his hold. Slowly, he was choking the life from the English champion.

23 Prostration and Plaudits

> *But do thou, O father Zeus, that rulest*
> *over the height of Atabyrium, grant honour*
> *to the hero who hath found fame for his*
> *prowess as a boxer; and do thou give him*
> *grace and reverence in the eyes of citizens,*
> *and of strangers too.*
>
> PINDAR (trans. Sir John Sandys)

Accounts of the battle, up to this point, broadly agreed on facts. What followed was transcribed for posterity with less accord. Most reporters, deprived of privileged positions in the chaos resulting from the police charge, missed some or all the remaining rounds. Henry Miles, swept through the ropes by encroaching spectators, struggled to the front, a protesting, red-faced figure 'among the driving crowd which swayed hither and thither in the broken ring'. Of three or four journalists nearby, all but one were non-specialists, impugned by Miles for their ignorance of boxing. 'Several,' he claimed later, 'wrote their accounts from hearsay.' Everything, admitted an American correspondent, had become 'inextricably confused'.

According to the *Herald*, Heenan was holding Sayers against the ropes by the neck 'as though he had it in a vice. There were cries of "That's murder!" and it really seemed as though Sayers's neck would be broken. . . . The referee had disappeared, and they were fighting amidst the crowd.' The *Herald* reckoned this to be the thirty-sixth round; another 'daily' fixed it as the thirty-eighth. Unquestionably, it was the thirty-seventh, as Miles and *Bell's Life* testified. Reported *The Times*:

Heenan had got Sayers's head under his left arm and, supporting himself by a stake with his right, held his opponent bent down as if he meant to strangle him. Sayers could no more free himself than if a mountain was on him. At last he got his left arm free and gave Heenan two dreadful blows on the face, covering them both with blood, but Heenan, without relaxing his hold, turned himself so as to get his antagonist's neck over the rope, and then leant on it with all his force. Sayers rapidly turned black in the face, and would have been strangled on the spot had both umpires not called simultaneously to cut the ropes. This was done at once, and both men fell heavily on the ground. The police now made a determined effort nearby, which those present seemed equally determined to prevent . . . the enclose was inundated by a dense mob which scarcely left the combatants six square feet to fight in. . . . This, on the whole, was unfair to Sayers, whose only chance lay in avoiding his antagonist, who, though as blind as a bat, still possessed immense strength.'

Miles disputed that the ropes were cut on instructions. As he saw it, they were lowered by Sayers's friends in the absence of the referee, an action at least in the spirit of the ring code, rule 28 stipulating that: 'Where a man shall have his antagonist across the ropes in such a position as to be helpless, and to endanger his life by strangulation or apoplexy, it shall be in the power of the referee to direct the seconds to take their man away, and thus conclude the round.' (As a result of the episode, the rule was revised to make it a foul to use the ropes or stakes as an aid to squeezing or hugging.)

Meanwhile, Dowling, seeing the ring submerged by spectators, had declared a cessation of hostilities. After two hours and six minutes, the fight officially was at an end. If this pronouncement ever penetrated the frantic human mass enclosing the fighters and their seconds, it was dismissed as a rumour flown to rob one or the other side of victory. Almost dementedly, the punters at the centre of the mob spurred their favourites to a last decisive effort. The arena was no more than a cockpit. Outside, less fanatical supporters were already streaming towards the trains. Others, including a resolute band of Americans, fought a holding action with the constables, convinced their man must win within minutes. Inside the wall of bodies, the prize-fight of the century, now a grotesque brawl, continued for five more rounds.

They were, as *Bell's Life* had it, an indescribable shambles. Sayers was almost too weary to stand up. 'His mouth and nose were dreadfully beaten, and the side of his head and forehead.' Heenan—'almost unrecognizable as a human being'—flailed his arms in desperation, falling over his opponent. Several times, he swung blows at spectators, mistaking them for Sayers. All attempts at time-keeping had gone, and intervals between bouts were arbitrary. In an extraordinary climax to these supplementary rounds, Heenan stumbled blindly into Harry Brunton and, believing him the English champion, knocked him down. Welsh, jumping forward to intervene, stopped a wild swing from the American, and crumpled. A third shape loomed before the 'Boy's' ineffective eyes. Trampling on the fallen British seconds, he lunged forward. This time, it was Sayers. A bizarre rally ensued, Heenan beating empty space around his adversary; Sayers practically incapable of throwing a punch without collapsing. Falling into each other's arms, they dropped to earth hopelessly.

It was their final throw. Dowling, having forced his way through the scrimmage, reaffirmed his order to end the fight, and the rearguard of the Fancy retreated towards the railway. The men had fought for two hours and twenty minutes, through forty-two rounds in all. Sayers had to be supported on either side and half-dragged away. Heenan, in a crazy display of bravura, sprinted a short distance before halting and dropping his face into tortured hands. A screen of British and American supporters covered their withdrawal from the meadow, but the outnumbered police did not follow. They, too, had had enough, and stopped to account their wounds. Miles, hurrying ahead of the crippled English bruiser, was in time to see Heenan lifted, undiscerning, into his compartment. By early afternoon, the excursionists were back in the metropolis.

*

The pugilists were put down, as a precaution, before reaching London Bridge, and taken in closed cabs to a pub in the Old Kent Road, The Swan, where the landlord, Ned Elgee, offered refreshments. Neither of the fighters was in a state to participate. Sayers, refusing to go to bed, slumped in a chair, unable to drink the champagne opened to toast his health. Gideon, crossing the street to Heenan's cab, found the 'Boy' seemingly unconscious, and advised his speedy removal to Osborne's hotel. There, he was confined to a darkened room, remaining in bed for forty-eight hours. On the morning after the contest, it was confirmed at Dowling's office in Norfolk Street that, due to the breaking of the ring and police intervention, the referee's decision was for a drawn battle. Possession of belt and money would depend on a second fight.

Soon afterwards, Superintendents Hannant and Durkin of the metropolitan police called at *Bell's Life*. Their purpose, by order of the commissioners and under direction of the Home Secretary, was to give Dowling notice that if Sayers and Heenan attempted to renew hostilities in any place subject to a Secretary of State's warrant, they would immediately be arrested; moreover, 'directions would be given to the proper authorities to indict them, and all persons concerned with the breach of peace already committed'. Dowling now refused to contemplate the arrangement of a further fight.

Public opinion in Britain was behind him. The men had done enough, declared the papers; a draw was a fair verdict. Elaborating the sentiment, Dowling suggested that the title should be shared; a replica belt made and awarded for each fighter. A vociferous minority disagreed. Some Americans who had attended the contest 'loudly and threateningly claimed the fight', asserted a New York correspondent, 'expressing a strong desire, after the affair was over, to whip any number of Englishmen'. Prejudice existed in the British camp. Miles considered Sayers to have had 'victory within his grasp' when the fight was stopped. Thackeray wrote in the *Cornhill* that 'the advantage was all on Mr Sayers's side'. But most people held the honours to be equal.

The *Saturday Review* expressed a general view:

If the British supporters did not witness exactly what they expected, they saw an even finer sight. Never in the annals of pugilism were skill, coolness, judgement, variety of resource, pluck and bottom displayed in such a wonderful degree. . . . Our own sovereign may be content to reckon Sayers among her subjects; to say, 'I trust I have within this realm / Ten thousand good as he' . . . An equal tribute is due to the gallant spirit which brought Heenan across the ocean. He has shown unflinching courage and tremendous strength.

Harry Hill summed up pithily: 'I don't believe there's anyone in the world could tell who was the better man. They were both worse off than I ever want to be, and both fought to win until the bitter end.'

Still, disappointments persisted a few days. On 19 April, before Heenan was fit to leave his bedroom, George Wilkes addressed a letter to the British press on the 'Boy's' behalf asserting that:

> ... neither he nor any person authorized to act for him had requested the referee to stop the fight. On the contrary, Heenan and his friends repeatedly protested against the invasion of the ropes and demanded that the fight should not be interrupted. . . . He wishes me to say that he feels sure that had not that occurrence taken place he would soon have made his victory manifest to the most prejudiced person on the ground. As to the suggestion kindly made by the editor of *Bell's Life* that Sayers and he should have a belt apiece, he begs me to say that, while he will cheerfully subscribe to a new testimonial for his brave and honourable adversary, Heenan will have none other than the one he came 9,000 miles [*sic*] to get, and believes he can win again if so required.

Sayers, as well as Heenan, voiced his readiness to fight again. That their words were ritualistic, divorced from realism, was evidenced by the ease with which both camps succumbed to Dowling's persuasion on meeting at his office on the 21st. 'After a while,' reported *The Times*, 'the friends of both men grew unanimous in their wishes that the affair might be settled in a kindly way.'

The powerless arm of the English champion, who was present, had 'got rather worse than better'. Heenan had yet to reveal himself. Neither can seriously have contemplated a repeat of their ordeal at Farnborough. Acclaim for both was enormous, while the money begging at benefits, exhibitions and other appearances far outweighed the likely profits of another fight. A substantial subscription and 'rapturous' welcome for Sayers, on visiting Chester and Liverpool at the month's end, indicated enviable prospects for the weeks ahead. Heenan, 'scarred and discoloured' but otherwise recovered, appeared in public again on 4 May, to be received almost as devotedly by the British public as was Sayers.

On 7 May, there appeared over Sayers's name in *The Times* a letter whose eloquent contribution to press relations clearly showed the hand of Gideon:

The period has arrived when it becomes my duty to thank the great British public for the patronage they have bestowed upon me. . . . I did my best for the land of my birth and dearest affections. I had opposed to me one worthy of me, and whose activity, rapidity and pluck it was no small task to encounter. Sprung from our own race, the Americans inherit our best qualities, and as our conflicts with them have in the progress of time ended in peace so may every bitterness engendered by the late struggle for the championship pass away forever. . . . To live to receive the kindly notice of that journal [*The Times*] which makes and unmakes reputations, which cheers the humble dwellings of the poor and makes tyrants tremble on their gilded thrones, is to have lived for a great and distinguished honour. Upon my own part, and that of my children, I humbly offer my most grateful thanks, and I trust, to whatever period Providence will extend my life, that no act of mine, either in private or in public life, will be unworthy of one who has received the notice of the *Times* newspaper. I remain, Sir, your obedient servant,

TOM SAYERS
Champion of England.

Nothing imagined could have restored the prestige of the prize-fighter more dramatically than the mill at Farnborough. Throughout the land—in respectable Victorian homes, as in respectable Victorian newspapers—millions who normally ranked pugilists with common criminals hailed an illiterate bruiser as a national hero. 'So long as manly sentiments and sheer British pluck are valued,' wrote Locker-Lampson, 'so long shall the name of Thomas Sayers, the Polydeuces of our country, be held in honour.' Foreign journals, as well as English, sang his praise. While the defence of England depended on chests as broad and arms as stout as those of Sayers, declared the *Constitutionnel*, the rights and liberties of that nation were well preserved. Theatres, music halls, race tracks, placed the champion on their free-lists. On Derby day that year, Princess Mary of Cambridge asked that Sayers should be presented to her. Shaking hands with him, and with Gideon, she gave the fighter a monogrammed handkerchief for his daughter, Sarah. It was the first recognition of the prize-ring by royalty since Victoria's accession.

On 30 May, the replica belts, worked in frosted silver by Hancock's, designers of the original, were presented at the Alhambra, London, by Wilkes and Dowling. 'America and England shake hands cordially today,' announced one paper. 'What the greatest diplomats and engineers have failed to achieve [*the new transatlantic cable had come to grief*] has been accomplished by the Benicia Boy and Tom Sayers, whose fame will descend to future generations.'

For the moment, adverse reaction was overwhelmed. But it was not silent. Many reporters at the great fight, while impressed by the spunk of the contestants, had deprecated the brutality of the sport. Hollingshead scarcely concealed his distaste. American correspondents declared their reluctance to attend the prize-ring in future. The French *Siècle* wrote of 'a barbarous and disgusting exhibition'. Lampson, despite his eulogy of Sayers, was appalled in time by the memory of the event. 'When I recall this battle, and Heenan's face, out of which all that was human had been pommelled, I cry, "Heaven forbid that the prize-ring should ever be revived in all its hideous and loathsome degradation!"'

Within days of the contest, questions were being asked at Westminster. 'More fun in the Commons about the fight,' exclaimed *Punch* in its Essence of Parliament column. 'Mr Ewart admitted but deplored the public interest, and wanted to know what power there was to suppress such doings, other than the police power to suppress riot.' Lovaine returned to the attack with an indictment of the South Eastern Railway company, whose directors had 'supposedly pledged themselves', he said, against abetting prize-fights. Revealing that a superintendent of the company had travelled with one of the special trains, Lovaine demanded to know whether the government had done anything about the matter, moving for copies to be produced 'of any correspondence which had passed between the government and the company'. The returns were ordered, but, if such correspondence existed, it never came to light. It did appear, however, that ticket sales for the excursion had realized 'between four and five thousand pounds'.

While the debate progressed, a subscription was being raised for Sayers by his London friends. Among the first to contribute a sovereign —the limit set for individual donations—was the head of the Government, Lord Palmerston.

24 The Mighty Fallen

> *Behind a cab-horse,*
> *Beyond Charing Cross;*
> *To see Miss Mazeppa*
> *Ride a wild horse.*
> *Rien on her figure*
> *As everyone knows—*
> *She shall have music*
> *If not any clothes.*
>   VICTORIAN JINGLE

The first suggestion in New York that news of the fight was approaching came with a smart hoax. On 25 April, a week after the battle, a counterfeit edition of the *Spirit of the Times* appeared on the streets containing a story, purportedly off the steamer *Vanderbilt*, of a tremendous contest at Mildenhall, Suffolk, on the 16th. According to its authors, this fictional tussle had resulted in Heenan snatching the 'double championship of the two hemispheres' in an hour and ten minutes. If the hoaxers lacked imagination on any score, it was simply in failing to print enough copies. Within minutes of newsvendors proclaiming the scoop in Irving Place, the audience had rushed wildly from a performance of *Martha* at the Academy and, joined by others in the neighbourhood, bought up the whole edition. 'What will Mr Wilkes say!' exclaimed a delighted fellow editor.

Three days later, Saturday, when the *Vanderbilt* actually docked, two tons of English newspapers, the largest amount ever shipped at one time, deluged America. The *New York Herald* made the running on Sunday with a special edition giving seven columns to the battle, including round-by-round reports from its own correspondent and *Bell's Life*. The front page carried a four-inch deck of headlines announcing 'The Great Contest for the Championship of the World', 'The Most Extraordinary Encounter in the Ring on Record', 'The Wonderful Endurance of the Two Men', and other marvels.

The presentation, reflecting the battle from both sides, was extremely fair—perhaps too fair for the liking of James Gordon Bennett, who followed it with a leading article some days later on American superiority, insisting that 'the Britons stopped the fight to save their money'. Certainly, America considered the result a moral victory. Throughout the republic, enthusiasts were filled with jubilation. Adah Menken, still billed as 'Mrs Heenan', was greeted with robust cheering at the start of her performance on the Monday. One reporter declared the Bowery patrons so excited that they forgot to munch peanuts.

'During her first piece, *Satan in Paris*, Mrs Heenan was constantly applauded, and when the curtain fell . . . boxes and gallery joined in a shout which was kept up until she made her appearance before the curtain, when the troubled element became calm and tranquil in breathless expectation of hearing a speech. But the actress was "too full for utterance" and retired amid a fresh outburst of cheers for Mr and Mrs Heenan.'

Heenan himself, profiting from exhibitions with Sayers in England, did not return to the States until August. Meanwhile, Menken continued to capitalize on his name. On her benefit night at the Bowery, the audience was treated to a piece entitled *The Benicia Boy in England*, one of several sketches inspired by the great fight. With his homecoming, she reverted promptly to her old style as Adah Isaacs Menken.

The east coast reception for Heenan was remarkable. Thousands of fight fans, and thousands more who had never been near a prize-ring, packed Jones's Wood, a popular open-air venue in New York, to greet their hero. 'After hosts of muscular Christians had paid homage to Saint Heenan,' quipped a contemporary, 'the great man showed what he did to Sayers by hammering a local pug-nosed expert called Ottignan.' One face was conspicuously absent from the cheering crowds. The *New York Tribune* searched in vain among the 'Boy's' entourage for 'the lady expected by some to reign Queen of the Lists, Miss Adah Isaacs Menken, who has claimed the distinction of being the wife of the great Heenan'.

It was a claim Heenan, for one, no longer recognized. Leaving her to Newell and other admirers, the 'Boy' moved on to Chicago, enjoying fresh adulation, a high life on the proceeds of public subscriptions, and the company of one Harriet Martin, whom Menken subsequently named in her 'divorce' petition. The excitement was short-lived. Heenan's summer of acclaim was abbreviated by another social novelty: the arrival in America that year of the Prince of Wales. Hopefully, the boxer's friends hinted at the prince's need for an American companion of Heenan's distinction. When Edward proved more interested in the daughters of elegant society than in a flash bruiser, the 'Boy' returned, disgruntled, to England, where he was to spend the years of the American Civil War variously travelling with a circus, operating as a bookmaker and following the prize-ring.

Among his close friends was Jem Mace, and in 1862 he watched the Mace–King championship fight at Thames Haven. Tom King, a former sailor and dock foreman of Stepney, East London, was the last legitimate champion of the old British prize-ring. His skill was not exceptional, but he was big and bold, and his honesty stood out at a time when prize-fighting was fast sliding into the hands of the tricksters and criminals who had always stalked the sidelines.

The immense publicity and rich profits attending the Farnborough battle had finally prompted the manipulators to take over. With them came the robber gangs. Fenchurch Street station was so infested with mobsters for the Mace–King excursion that the bruisers detailed to protect the public were overwhelmed, and, in some instances, themselves plundered. Bob Travers was attacked and his pockets stripped. Many fans, too frightened to continue, returned home. The fight, unlike a lot by this time, was genuine. Mace was beaten by his own over-confidence. After eighteen rounds, his supremacy had pushed the odds to 6 to 1 against Tom King. Then, in the nineteenth, Mace opened himself to a stunning cross-counter from which he never recovered. Two rounds later, his corner threw up the sponge.

King's clumsiness tempted Heenan to challenge him. Extravagant living had softened the American, but his name was still a draw in England. The match, promoted as the natural sequel to the great fight, and for unprecedented stakes of a thousand pounds a side, aroused suspicions from the outset. Both fighters immediately made trading capital of the publicity by touring the provinces. It was widely assumed that the organizers would cash in on the excursion tickets, increasing their fortune by rigging the fight itself. The contest eventually took place in May 1863, at Wadhurst, Kent, before an audience smaller than that seen at Farnborough, but still sizeable. It proved, as many had predicted, a fiasco. Sayers appeared as a second for Heenan. Attired in fur cap, yellow jacket and jackboots, he created a considerable diversion, less for his flamboyant dress than his sickly and bibulous aspect.

'How are the mighty fallen!' wrote Henry Miles. 'Tom was no more equal to his task than a child. During the fight, he looked in strange bewilderment at King and Heenan, and when the Benicia Boy required assistance his second was perfectly helpless.'

Heenan, though restored to something of his erstwhile fitness by training, produced little of his old form. According to one report, the fighting 'more resembled a turn-up of two angry navvies than the tactics of skilled boxers. The exchanges were severe, but most of the blows seemed given at random.' Later, Heenan maintained he had been drugged, a claim many who were present thought plausible. Like Mace, he fell to a crippling punch in the nineteenth round and withdrew after struggling through another bout or two.

The contest plunged prize-fighting to new depths of disrepute. Within a few years of its sensational renaissance in 1860, the bare-knuckle game was once more a dying sport. At last, the British public swung solidly behind the anti-fight laws, supporting magistracy and police. Ironically, outrage centred less on the ferocity—which diminished as more and more contests became a sham—than on the crooked exploitation of the ring to dupe punters and enthusiasts. The pantomime disgusted alike the true Fancy and its old foes. The prize-ring in Britain was down and very nearly out. With the emergence of the Amateur Athletic club and the Queensberry rules in the late sixties, the infant of modern boxing may be said to have succeeded the deposed code.

For those who recalled the more admirable of pugilism's qualities, and the integrity of its best men, the great fight of 1860 remained a fitting climax to an epoch. The débâcle at Wadhurst did not extinguish the affection of many Englishmen for Heenan. But it ended his days as a champion. Thereafter, he lived on gambling, his limited wits and the loyalty of Cusick, who continued to dream of a come-back.

As Heenan's celebrity faded, so Menken's star soared in the firmament. In 1864, *Mazeppa* opened in London. The sensation sustained the 'Naked Lady' not only as the talk of the season, but for much of the coming year. She lived like a duchess. 'I had an engagement to ride horseback in the Park today at 12,' she wrote Edwin James. 'And you know the Prince is again in Rotten Row, and what woman of spirit, or taste, would keep away if she could possibly get out, and more especially if Poole [*the famous Savile Row habit-makers*] had just sent home her new and beautiful riding habit? Dark blue embroidered with silver, *à la militaire*, long white plumes, etc., etc.'

Her main complaint seemed to be that London's critics and writers, the men she took care to cultivate, were elderly. 'I go round with old men. They are generally "slow". However, they are quite jolly.' Younger, faster admirers were favoured in her dressing-rooms. Heenan, a frequent attender of her performances, patched up their relationship to the extent of sharing her cigars and refreshments. The luxury of her life might have tempted him further, but Menken merely played with him. Dubbing him 'Lord Carmel', after his second name, she boasted that he had abandoned another woman (seemingly Sarah Stevens, a showgirl who became his partner for a short time) on her behalf. 'She has gone to California with the express understanding never to write or see his lordship again. He is disgusted with her, since our reconciliation.'

The reconciliation was of short span. While Menken's triumphal progress led to Europe, Heenan, down on his luck, returned to New York after the Civil War and became involved again with the City Hall muscle gangs. The step put his fortunes beyond restoration. 'Boss' William Tweed was in power. When his gigantic thefts and misuses of public money were exposed, Heenan was among the small fry charged with corruption. By 1873, two years after Tweed's downfall, the 'Benicia Boy' was destitute; a thirty-eight-year-old pug reduced to sparring for a livelihood. Cusick was still with him. At the end of summer, they set out by Union Pacific to seek better things in California, the state which had given Heenan a start, and his sobriquet.

The 'Boy's' physique belied his actual health. At the time of the

Farnborough battle, John Hollingshead had made a prophetic observation. The fighters, he had written, looked firm and muscular, but many professional pugilists harboured the seeds of fatal illnesses. Across the Bad Lands and approaching the Rockies, Heenan took sick. On the morning of 25 October, he died in Cusick's arms at Green River Station, near Rawlins, Wyoming. The New York papers gave the news a bare mention. On file, his career was not distinguished. Curiously, though the best American pugilist of his period, Heenan had never won a championship contest, losing two of his three attempts to fighters of less aptitude. His reputation rested solely on the mill at Farnborough.

That it was arguably the greatest battle ever seen in a boxing ring meant little a decade, and a civil war, later. If anything, his death stirred more memories in England than America. When the news reached London in November, the press recalled the 'Boy' kindly, and *Punch* published an epitaph:

> *Here Heenan lies, the stalwart son of Troy,*
> *But better known as the Benicia Boy.*
> *With him, in '60, bold Tom Sayers fought—*
> *The battle ended as it didn't ought . . .*
> *But this we do say, both was noble fellows,*
> *As good as Virgil's Dares and Entellus.*

25 L'Envoy

To-day Spring tints the little copse
Unearthly shades of green.
The turf treads firm beneath the feet;
The pulse throbs with a quicker beat;
For on this hallowed ground and sweet
A perfect fight has been.

ANON.

Around the clubs of London, at Westminster, the Stock Exchange, Lloyd's and Mark Lane, sovereigns passed hands for Tom Sayers until, within weeks of the great fight, it was known that three thousand guineas had been raised and invested in government stock for the champion. The conditions attached to the money by the committee of well-wishers who handled it were that Sayers should receive the interest on the investment (4½%) during his life, provided he did not fight again. The paramount concern of Gideon, and other friends, was that the champion should not dissipate, nor be robbed of the windfall, nor be coerced into the ring in decline, to end his days, like so many bruisers, on the scrapheap. At his death, the capital was to be divided equally between his two children, young Tom and Sarah, payable on majority.

The result was a modest but guaranteed income for Sayers, on top of which he had a considerable sum from benefits and appearances throughout the country, as well as a share of the rail excursion profits. During the summer of 1860, he was a popular figure at race meetings and other events in the social calendar, smartly dressed and usually accompanied by Gideon, who kept the sharks from his artless ward. In August, Gideon's departure for France presaged trouble for the Camden pug. Already, Sayers had made a number of lucrative guest appearances with Howes and Cushing's circus, a travelling outfit managed by an acquaintance of Gideon named Jem Myers. The attraction of horses and other animals, the free and easy circus life, fascinated the champion. When he was offered shares in Howes and Cushing's, and later the chance to buy it outright, he jumped in.

Without Gideon's guidance, Sayers was a gullible investor. The circus was failing, squeezed by Lord George Sanger and other forceful rivals, but Myers insisted that Sayers's name and participation would draw the crowds. Trustfully, the new proprietor kept Myers as his manager and employed Cushing as adviser. Sayers did his best. In garish costume, sporting a large cigar, he preceded the circus to town in a triumphal chariot drawn by two mules, Peter and Barney. He even appeared in the ring as a clown—'the most melancholy clown,' according to a contemporary, 'who ever cried "*Allez vous*, here we are again!"' His attachment to the animals was sincere, but Sayers was no more a showman than a businessman. Twelve months later, the circus was finished; props, carriages and livestock sold to settle liabilities.

By the time Gideon returned in 1862, Sayers had run through his own money. Worse, his health had begun to break. He had lost weight. He had discovered an ominous deposit on his polished circus boots which transpired to be a residual of sugar-saturated urine. The symptoms were accompanied soon by excessive thirst which, in his anxiety, Sayers sought to quench with draughts of beer and brandy. Increasingly, he withdrew from public sight. On the rare occasions when he resumed the limelight—among them, to second for Heenan at Wadhurst—his drinking was put down to frivolous extravagance. 'Unable to fall back on the pleasures of a cultivated mind from want of education,' wrote Miles, 'he cast off all those restraints which had secured for him health and victory, and plunged into excesses of living —late hours and dissipation. Nature's laws are not to be broken with impunity . . .' Miles was confusing effect and cause.

Following the Heenan–King fight, Gideon insisted that Sayers saw a doctor. The diagnosis was diabetes; the prognosis, then, unhopeful. Any work was out of the question. Only by strict dieting, it seemed, could fatality be deferred. Sayers lived quietly with his sister in Claremont Square, driving out when he was strong enough in his dog cart with his son and daughter, and his mastiff, Lion. In February 1865, lung infection accompanied a crisis which was averted for the time by careful nursing, and in spring he was well enough to visit his old home-town, Brighton. There, he spent his last summer, returning late August to London and a serious relapse. By mid-October, Sayers was beyond help from his doctor, consolation confined to visits from the assistant chaplain of St Pancras workhouse. The ex-champion endured three more weeks of agony, intermittently unconscious, before dying on the evening of 9 November.

It was the Lord Mayor of London's day. At six o'clock, the moment of Sayers's death, Lord Palmerston, the Gladstones, and other dis-tinguished guests were arriving at Guildhall for the mayor's banquet. In the police cells of the city lay a crew more familiar to Sayers and the Fancy—the professional pick-pockets arrested among the gala crowds in Newgate, Farringdon Street, Fleet Street and Cheapside. Next morning, Mr Alderman Abbiss devoted upwards of an hour at Mansion House police court to sentencing those convicted of stealing watches and purses. A rueful 'fine-wirer' named Daniels declared he would rather have faced the 'Benicia Boy'.

Neither Heenan nor Sayers lived to see forty years. The latter was thirty-nine at his death, a wasted ghost of the gladiator hailed at Farnborough. A loyal crowd of admirers, together with others merely curious, attended his interment at Highgate, North London. Here, at the instigation of a party of old friends, was raised on the grave a memorial bearing the champion's profile and a sculpture of his dog, Lion, in watchful repose. There was no epitaph. Sayers's own descrip-tion of the sensation he experienced after heavy fighting might have filled the spot: 'My head clears. The pain goes. I feel like I've exchanged my body for a new one.'

On the afternoon of 1 December, an auction sale at Camden Town of 'the whole of the trophies and other effects, animate and inanimate, of the late Tom Sayers,' fetched slightly less than five hundred pounds. The proceeds were made over, by bequest, to nis father. Among other items, the belt won at Farnborough realized £33. 12s.; the circus mule Barney, for whom Sayers had a special affection, fetched £13; his dun driving pony made £23. The highest bid of the sale was for 'lot 103, the well known English mastiff, Lion'. Most constant of the champion's companions, the dog was knocked down for thirty-nine guineas to the landlord of the Welsh Harp tavern, Hendon.

There remained the three thousand guineas invested for the children. At Sayers's death, his son was fourteen, still at boarding school; his daughter in her seventeenth year. In 1870, Sarah would have qualified, by the original intention, for half the sum. But in 1868, Sayers's widow, the elder Sarah, took legal action to obtain the estate for herself and her Aldridge children. For the first time, it became public knowledge that Sayers's own children were legally illegitimate, and that the subsequent offspring of Mrs Sayers had been registered as her husband's. Nothing stood between Mrs Sayers and success save the improbability of proving that Sayers could not have fathered her later sons. There was, found the Master of Rolls, insufficient evidence to show as much.

Though award of the inheritance to Sayers's wife and the Aldridge children frustrated the Camden fighter's fondest wish, young Tom and Sarah still had a champion. Gideon, sickened by the outcome, arranged assistance and helped them to fruitful independence. Sarah married and lived in Newcastle. Tom, in a move once contemplated by his namesake, emigrated to Australia, achieving success in business. In 1891, after further litigation, he gained possession of his father's grave. It had fallen into sad neglect. Locker-Lampson, who visited Highgate shortly before his own death, recalled chatting with the cemetery custodian.

'He spoke with pardonable complacency of the many distinguished people who had been buried within the precincts. . . . "And then," said he, "we have another that used to be a deal talked about. You've heard, perhaps, of Tom Sayers, the fightin' man?" '

Lampson had.

'Alas, poor Tom!' he reflected.

APPENDIXES

I 'The Combat of Sayerius and Heenanus'

The following is the full text of the poem, generally attributed to Thackeray, which appeared in Punch *on 28 April 1860. A parody of Macaulay's legend of Horatius in the* Lays of Ancient Rome, *it is supposedly recounted by an ancient gladiator to his great-grandchildren.*

A Lay of Ancient London

Close round my chair, my children,
And gather at my knee,
The while your mother poureth
The Old Tom in my tea;
What while your father quaffeth
His meagre Bordeaux wine—
Twas not on such potations
Were reared these thews of mine.
Such drinks came in the very year—
Methinks I mind it well—
That the great fight of HEENANUS
With SAYERIUS befell.*

These knuckles then were iron,
This biceps like a cord,
This fist shot from the shoulder
A bullock would have floored.
CRAWLEIUS his Novice,
They used to call me then

* Cheap French wines were first admitted to Britain at low duty in 1860.

In the Domus Savilliana*
Among the sporting men.
There, on benefit occasions,
The gloves I oft put on,
Walking round to show my muscle
When the set-to was done;
While ringing in the arena
The showered denarii fell,
That told CRAWLEIUS' Novice
Had used his mauleys well.

Tis but some sixty years since
The times of which I speak,
And yet the words I'm using
Will sound to you like Greek.
What know ye, race of milksops,
Untaught of the P.R.,
What stopping, lunging, countering,
Fibbing or rallying are?
What boots to use the *lingo*,
When you have lost the *thing*?
How paint to you the glories
Of BELCHER, CRIBB or SPRING—
To *you*, whose sire turns up his eyes
At mention of the Ring?

Yet, in despite of all the jaw
And gammon of this time,
That brands the art of self-defence—
Old England's art—as crime,
From off mine ancient memories
The rust of time I'll shake,
Your youthful bloods to quicken
And your British pluck to wake;
I know it only slumbers,
Let cant do what it will,

* Saville House, Leicester Square, where sparring exhibitions were held.

The British bull-dog will be
The British bull-dog still.
Then gather to your grandsire's knee,
The while his tale is told
How SAYERIUS and HEENANUS
Milled in those days of old

The Beaks and Blues were watching
Agog to stop the mill,
As we gathered to the station
In April morning chill;
By two and threes, by fours and tens,
To London Bridge we drew;
For we had had 'the office'
That were good men and true;
And saving such, the place of fight
Was ne'er a man that knew.
From East, from West, from North and South,
The London Fancy poured,
Down to the sporting cabman,
Up to the sporting lord;
From the Horseshoe in Tichbourne Street
Sharp OWEN SWIFT was there;
JEM BURN had left the Rising Sun,
All in the Street of Air;
LANGHAM had cut the Cambrian
With tough old ALEC REID,
And towering high above the crowd
Shone BEN CAUNT's fragrant weed;
Not only fighting covies,
But sporting swells besides—
Dukes, Lord, M.P.s and Guardsmen,
With county Beaks for guides;
And tongues that sway our Senators,
And hands the pen that wield,
Were cheering on the Champions
Upon that morning's field.

And hark! the bell is ringing,
The engine puffs amain,
And through the dark towards Brighton
On shrieks the tearing train;
But turning off where Reigate
Unites the clustering lines,
By poultry-haunted Dorking
A devious course it twines,
By Wootton, Shier and Guildford,
Across the winding Wey,
Till by heath-girded Farnborough
Our doubling course we stay,
Where Aldershot lay snoring
All in the morning grey,
Nor dreamed the Camp what combat
Should be fought here today.

The stakes are pitched, the ropes are rove,
The men have ta'en their stand;
HEENANUS wins the toss for place
And takes the eastward hand;
CUSSICCIUS and MACDONALDUS
Upon the BOY attend;
SAYERIUS owns BRUNTONIUS
With JEM WELSHIUS for friend.
And each upon the other now
A curious eye may throw,
And from the seconds' final rub
In buff at length they show,
And from their corners to the scratch
Move stalwartly and slow.

Then each his hand stretched forth to grasp
His foeman's fives in friendly clasp;
Each felt his balance trim and true—
Each up to square his mauleys threw—

Each tried his best to draw his man—
The feint, the dodge, the opening plan,
Till right and left SAYERIUS tried—
HEENANUS' grin proclaimed him wide;
Then shook his nut—a lead essayed,
Nor reached SAYERIUS' watchful head.
At length each left is sudden flung,
We hear the ponderous thud,
And from each tongue the news was rung,
SAYERIUS hath first blood!
Adown HEENANUS' Roman nose
Freely the tell-tale claret flows,
While stern SAYERIUS' forehead shows
That in the interchange of blows
HEENANUS' aim was good!
Again each iron mauley swung,
And loud the counter-hitting rung,
Till breathless both, and wild with blows,
Fiercely they grappled for a close;
One moment in close hug they swing,
Hither and thither round the ring,
Then from HEENANUS' clinch of brass,
SAYERIUS, smiling, slips to grass!

I trow mine ancient breath would fail
To follow through the fight,
Each gallant round's still changing tale,
Each feat of left and right.
How through two well-fought hours and more,
Through bruise, and blow, and blood,
Like sturdy bull-dogs as they were,
Those well-matched heroes stood.
How nine times in that desperate mill
HEENANUS, in his strength,
Knocked stout SAYERIUS off his pins,
And laid him all at length;
But how in each succeeding round

SAYERIUS smiling came,
With head as cool, and wind as sound,
As his first moment on the ground,
Still confident and game.
How from HEENANUS' sledge-like fist,
Striving a smasher to resist,
SAYERIUS' stout right arm gave way,
Yet the maimed hero still made play,
And when in-fighting threatened ill,
Was nimble in out-fighting still—
Still did his own maintain—
In mourning put HEENANUS' glims,
Till blinded eyes and helpless limbs
The chances squared again.
How blind HEENANUS, in despite
Of bleeding face and waning sight,
So gallantly kept up the fight,
That not a man could say
Which of the two twere wise to back,
Or on which side some random crack
Might not decide the day;
And leave us—whoso won the prize—
Victor and vanquished, in all eyes,
And equal meed to pay.

Two hours and more the fight had sped,
Near unto ten it drew,
But still opposed—one-armed to blind—
They stood, those dauntless two.
Ah, me! that I have lived to hear
Such men as ruffians scorned,
Such deeds of valour 'brutal' called,
Canted, preached-down and mourned!
Ah! that these old eyes ne'er again
A gallant mill shall see!
No more behold the ropes and stakes,
With colours flying free!

But I forget the combat—
How shall I tell the close?
That left the Champion's belt in doubt
Between those well-matched foes?
Fain would I shroud the tale in night—
The meddling Blues that thrust in sight—
The ring-keeper o'erthrown;
The broken ropes—th' encumbered fight—
HEENANUS' sudden blinded flight—
SAYERIUS pausing, as he might,
Just when ten minutes, used aright,
Had made the day his own.
Alas! e'en those brighter days
We still had Beaks and Blues—
Still canting rogues, their mud to fling,
On self-defence, and on the Ring,
And fistic art abuse!
And twas such varmint had the power
The Champions' fight to stay,
And leave unsettled to this hour
The honours of the day!
But had those honours rested—
Divided as was due,
SAYERIUS and HEENANUS
Had cut the Belt in two.

And now my fists are feeble,
And my blood is thin and cold,
But tis better than Old Tom to me
To recall those days of old.
And may you, my great-grandchildren,
That gather round my knee,
Ne'er see worse men, nor iller times
Than I and mine might be,
Though England then had prize-fighters—
Even reprobates like me.

II 'Bendy's Sermon'

*Sir Arthur Conan Doyle reflected the Bendigo legend in the following lines,
which achieved considerable popularity in their time. They are reprinted by
permission of Baskervilles Investments Ltd.*

You didn't know of Bendigo! Well, that knocks me out!
Who's your board school teacher? What's he been about?
Chock-a-block with fairy-tales—full of useless cram,
And never heard of Bendigo, the pride of Nottingham!

Bendy's short for Bendigo. You should see him peel!
Half of him was whalebone, half of him was steel,
Fightin' weight eleven ten, five foot nine in height,
Always ready to oblige if you want a fight.

I could talk of Bendigo from here to kingdom come,
I guess before I ended you would wish your dad was dumb,
I'd tell you how he fought Ben Caunt, and how the Deaf 'un fell,
But the game is done, and the men are gone—and maybe it's as
     well.

Bendy he turned Methodist—he said he felt a call,
He stumped the country preaching and you bet he filled the hall,
If you seed him in the pulpit, a'bleatin' like a lamb,
You'd never know bold Bendigo, the pride of Nottingham.

His hat was like a funeral, he'd got a waiter's coat,
With a hallelujah collar and a choker round his throat,
His pals would laugh and say in chaff that Bendigo was right
In takin' on the devil, since he'd no one else to fight.

But he was very earnest, improvin' day by day,
A-workin' and a-preachin' just as his duty lay,
But the devil he was waitin', and in the final bout
He hit him hard below his guard and knocked poor Bendy out.

Now I'll tell you how it happened. He was preachin' down at
    Brum,
He was billed just like a circus, you should see the people come,
The chapel it was crowded, and in the foremost row
There was half a dozen bruisers who'd a grudge at Bendigo.

There was Tommy Platt of Bradford, Solly Jones of Perry Bar,
Long Connor from the Bull Ring, the same wot drew with Carr,
Jack Ball the fightin' gunsmith, Joe Murphy from the Mews,
And Iky Moss, the bettin' boss, the Champion of the Jews.

A very pretty handful a-sittin' in a string,
Full of beer and impudence, ripe for anything,
Sittin' in a string there, right under Bendy's nose,
If his message was for sinners, he could make a start on those.

Soon he heard them chaffin': 'Hi, Bendy! Here's a go!'
'How much are you coppin' by this Jump to Glory show?'
'Stow it, Bendy! Left the ring! Mighty spry of you!
Didn't everybody know the ring was leavin' you?'

Bendy fairly sweated as he stood above and prayed,
'Look down, O Lord, and grip me with a strangle hold!' he said.
'Fix me with a strangle hold! Put a stop on me!
I'm slippin', Lord, I'm slippin' and I'm clingin' hard to Thee!'

But the roughs they kept on chaffin' and the uproar it was such
That the preacher in the pulpit might be talkin' double Dutch,
Till a workin' man he shouted out, a-jumpin' to his feet,
'Give us a lead, your reverence, and heave 'em in the street.'

Then Bendy says, 'Good Lord, since first I left my sinful ways,
Thou knowest that to Thee alone I've given up my days,
But now, dear Lord'—and here he laid his Bible on the shelf—
'I'll take with your permission just five minutes for myself.'

He vaulted from the pulpit like a tiger from a den,
They say it was a lovely sight to see him floor his men;
Right and left, and left and right, straight and true and hard,
Till the Ebenezer Chapel looked more like a knacker's yard.

Platt was standin' on his back and lookin' at his toes,
Solly Jones of Perry Bar was feelin' for his nose,
Connor of the Bull Ring had all that he could do
Rakin' for his ivories that lay about the pew.

Jack Ball the fightin' gunsmith was in a peaceful sleep,
Joe Murphy lay across him, all tied up in a heap,
Five of them was twisted in a tangle on the floor,
And Iky Moss, the bettin' boss, had sprinted for the door.

Five repentant fightin' men, sitting in a row,
Listenin' to words of grace from Mister Bendigo,
Listenin' to his reverence—all as good as gold,
Pretty little baa-lambs, gathered to the fold.

So that's the way that Bendy ran his mission in the slum,
And preached the Holy Gospel to the fightin' men of Brum,
'The Lord,' said he, 'has given me His message from on high,
And if you interrupt Him, I will know the reason why.'

But to think of all your schoolin', clean wasted, thrown away,
Darned if I can make out what you're learnin' all the day,
Grubbin' up old fairy-tales, fillin' up with cram,
And didn't know of Bendigo, the pride of Nottingham!

Bibliographical Note

In setting out to connect some fragments of the past in a sporting narrative, it has not been a purpose of the author to provide detailed references. Little work of a painstaking nature on the Victorian prize-ring exists in book form, and an index of the journalistic snippets and fusty records consulted in preparing these pages would be as tedious as it would be interminable. Most of the leading London and New York journals of the period provide limited information on the subject, as do some provincial newspapers, and a few from Paris. Items and writers of special interest have been mentioned in the text. Among other sources, railway company minutes, quarter session records, county constabulary accounts, Home Office papers and parliamentary debates contain occasional references to prize-fights. A rare, and unfortunately brief, article on rail fight-excursions appeared in the *Railway Magazine*, June 1959, by G. R. Mahon.

The boxing scene has produced few chroniclers with the knowledge and flair of Pierce Egan or A. J. Liebling. On the whole, the reader in search of Victorian pugilism must tolerate the juvenile jargon which passed for ringside reporting at the period. Its facetiousness is tedious, but its basic accuracy—so far as may be verified by comparing independent accounts of any one event—is respectable. Volume 3 of Miles's *Pugilistica* offers contemporary reports in this style of many of the major contests from the time of Bendigo to Tom King. Biographies of the champions, when such works existed, were inferior. Hurriedly produced on the demise of their subjects, they consisted typically of old fight reports strung together with verbal padding. In this category, regrettably, are the biographies of Sayers (*Tom Sayers, Sometime Champion of England*, by Miles) and Heenan (*The Life and Battles of J. C. Heenan*, by Edwin James). The position was partly redressed in respect of Sayers by a modest, but welcome, addition of recent years, *The Life of Tom Sayers*, by Tom Langley.

For contemporary prize-ring reporting at its best, it is necessary to go back to the Regency and Pierce Egan, the outstanding sports journalist of the bare-knuckle age. That the essentials of pugilism altered little between the time of Egan and the Farnborough fight make his inspired sketches the more worth reading. Of *Boxiana*, his best-selling collection of fight pieces, *Blackwood's Magazine* asserted: 'The man who has not read *Boxiana* is ignorant of the power of the English language.' More truthfully, it might be said that Egan created his own language; a racy, slangy, original lingo, threaded with almost surrealistic images, which belonged entirely to himself and the Fancy. J. C. Reid's *Bucks and Bruisers* should be read for a first-rate portrait of Egan and his period. *Fistiana*, by Dowling, takes events up to 1841, containing, among other things, a 'chronology of the ring' which lists many early bruisers and the results of their battles.

The fundamental and dramatic nature of bare-fist fighting has been used effectively in a great deal of literature, but fictional accounts of the prize-ring are seldom authentic. Dickens's portrait of the 'Game Chicken' in *Dombey and Son* is, as George Bernard Shaw asserts, a pious caricature based on ignorance of the species—a comment, ironically, that equally fits Shaw's own pugilist in *Cashel Byron's Profession*, a novel with some pertinent observations on the exploitation of bruisers, but little realism. Hazlitt's account of the duel between Bill Neat (he misspells the name) and the 'Gas Man' in *The Fight* is engrossing yet questionable. Hazlitt's knowledge of pugilism was slight. Quiller-Couch, R. D. Blackmore and Thomas Hughes memorably described fist-fights between boys, and Conan Doyle wrote some enjoyable short stories about pugilists (in *Tales of the Ring and Camp*), but none claimed an intimate connection with the prize-ring. George Borrow knew more of fighting men at first hand, and his scenes in *Lavengro* are convincing. In *The Bare-Knuckle Breed*, Louis Golding sets out to tell the stories of some famous fights with less emphasis on facts than rollicking inventiveness.

On the association of crime and vice with the prize-ring, it is worth reading Kellow Chesney's excellent *The Victorian Underworld*, while those interested in the career of Adah Menken should consult Bernard

Falk's *The Naked Lady*, a fulsome but informative biography. As a guide to further reading, the following list comprises books on, or touching, various aspects of the great fight, its *dramatis personae* and background:

BENNETT, A. R. *London and Londoners in the Eighteen-Fifties and Sixties.* London, 1924.

BERKLEY, HON. GRANTLEY. *My Life and Recollections.* London, 1865.

BOURNE, GEORGE. *William Smith, Potter and Farmer.* London, 1920.

BROWN, H. C. *The Story of Old New York.* New York, 1934.

CHANCELLOR, E. BERESFORD. *Annals of the Strand.* London, 1912.

CHESNEY, KELLOW. *The Victorian Underworld.* London, 1970.

CUNNINGHAM, G. H. *London.* London, 1927.

DAY, J. WENTWORTH. *Inns of Sport.* London, 1949.

DICEY, A. V. *Law and Public Opinion in England during the Nineteenth Century.* London, 1914.

DOWLING, F. *Fistiana, or the Oracle of the Ring.* London, 1841.

EGAN, PIERCE. *Boxiana, or Sketches of Pugilism.* London, 1813.

FALK, BERNARD. *The Naked Lady.* London and New York, 1934.

GOLDING, LOUIS. *The Bare-Knuckle Breed.* London, 1952.

GOLESWORTHY, MAURICE. *Encyclopaedia of Boxing.* London, 1960.

GREENWOOD, JAMES. *The Seven Curses of London.* London, 1869.

HALDANE, ROBERT A. *The Story of the Prize Ring.* London and New York, 1948.

HARDING, W. E. *John C. Heenan, His Life and Battles.* New York, 1881.

HOUSE, HUMPHREY. *The Dickens World.* London, 1942.

JAMES, E. *The Life and Battles of J. C. Heenan.* New York, 1879.

JOHNSTON, ALEXANDER. *Ten and Out! The Complete Story of the Prize Ring in America.* New York, 1927.

KENT, WILLIAM. *Mine Host London.* London, 1948.

LANGLEY, TOM. *The Life of Tom Sayers.* London, 1973.

LIEBLING, A. J. *The Sweet Science.* London and New York, 1956.

LOCKER-LAMPSON, FREDERICK. *My Confidences.* London, 1896.

LYNCH, BOHUN. *The Prize Ring.* London, 1925.

MAXTED, HARRY. *The Story of the Prize Ring.* London, 1949.

MILES, H. D. *Pugilistica* (3 vols). London, 1906.

—— *Tom Sayers, Sometime Champion of England.* London, 1866.

MYERS, G. *The History of Tammany Hall*. New York, 1917.

NICHOLSON, RENTON. *Rogue's Progress: The Autobiography of 'Lord Chief Baron' Nicholson* (ed. J. L. Bradley). London, 1966.

ODELL, G. C. D. *Annals of the New York Stage* (7 vols). New York, 1927–31.

REID, J. C. *Bucks and Bruisers; Pierce Egan and Regency England*. London, 1971.

SHEPHERD, T. B. *The Noble Art, a Boxing Anthology*. London, 1950.

THOMSON, DAVID. *England in the Nineteenth Century*. London, 1950.

TOBIAS, J. J. *Crime and Industrial Society in the 19th Century*. London, 1967.

WHITE, H. P. *A Regional History of the Railways of Great Britain*; vol. 2, *Southern England*. London, 1961.

WRIGHT, THOMAS. *The Great Unwashed*. London, 1868.

Index